THE PENGUIN CLASSICS

FOUNDER EDITOR (1944–64): E. V. RIEU

PRESENT EDITORS:
Betty Radice and Robert Baldick

L191

D1634516

NOT TO BE REMOVED
FROM THE LIBRARY

WITHDRAWN FROM
THE LIBRARY

UNIVERSITY OF
WINCHESTER

KA 0164506 4

TERENCE

PHORMIO

AND OTHER PLAYS

TRANSLATED WITH AN INTRODUCTION
BY BETTY RADICE

PENGUIN BOOKS

Penguin Books Ltd, Harmondsworth, Middlesex, England
Penguin Books Inc., 3300 Clipper Mill Road,
Baltimore, Md 21211, U.S.A.
Penguin Books Australia Ltd, Ringwood, Victoria, Australia

—

This translation first published 1967

—

Copyright © Betty Radice, 1967

—

Application for permission to perform these
plays should be made to the League of Dramatists,
84 Drayton Gardens, London s w 10

—

Made and printed in Great Britain
by Richard Clay (The Chaucer Press) Ltd,
Bungay, Suffolk
Set in Monotype Bembo

KING ALFRED'S COLLEGE
WINCHESTER

REF

872
TER | 40809

This book is sold subject to the condition
that it shall not, by way of trade or otherwise,
be lent, re-sold, hired out, or otherwise circulated
without the publisher's prior consent in any form of
binding or cover other than that in which it is
published and without a similar condition
including this condition being imposed
on the subsequent purchaser

CONTENTS

INTRODUCTION   7

THE GIRL FROM ANDROS
    [ANDRIA]   15

THE SELF-TORMENTOR
    [HEAUTON TIMORUMENOS]   75

PHORMIO   139

BIBLIOGRAPHY   203

INTRODUCTION

THE Roman playwright Terence (Publius Terentius Afer) wrote six comedies before he left Rome in 160 B.C., in his twenty-fifth year, and never returned. All six are extant, along with the author's prologues (the earliest example in Latin of a literary apologia) and notices of the first productions of the plays of a later date. The problems connected with Terence's life and early death were discussed in an earlier volume* and something was said there about his influence on European drama. Here we might look back to his predecessors and his debt to his Greek models.

Menander (342–291 B.C.) and his contemporaries fixed the style of Greek New Comedy which took the place of the old topical, satirical comedy of the fifth century, made famous by Aristophanes. Athens was then no longer a great power and a politically active democracy; money-making through commerce or professional soldiering were the new outlets, and the common man's interests were largely domestic and personal. This is reflected in New Comedy, where love themes and their attendant problems prevail, and the characters are individuals engaged in a battle of wits with friends and neighbours. No interest is expressed in the politics of the day, with the result that New Comedy dispenses with topical allusions and is free to be more cosmopolitan and show the social barriers less rigidly defined. There are new feelings abroad of humanity and elementary justice, a suggestion that a slave might be as good as his master, and in many ways the society presented is

* *The Brothers and Other Plays*, tr. Betty Radice (Penguin Classics, 1965). Suetonius' *Life* of Terence is included in an appendix.

more civilized, though more disillusioned, than any hitherto
known. Menander's plays helped to spread the ideal of Hel-
lenism as a form of culture distinguishing the civilized Greek
world from 'barbarism', an ideal which had been expressed
as early as 380 in the *Panegyricus* of Isocrates. They also took
the place of the Euripidean form of tragedy, where themes of
human interest alone were already replacing the grand tragic
subjects of man's relations with the state and with the gods.
Menander has certainly far more in common with Euripides
than he has with Aristophanes.

New Comedy also reflects the current interest in character-
types, best illustrated by the *Characters* of Theophrastus (371–
288), which were possibly written as part of a treatise on
comedy and to some extent bridge the gap between the larger-
than-life fantasy figures of Aristophanes and Menander's more
realistic ordinary men.* The idea of classifying people goes
back at least as far as Aristotle's *Ethics* and his *Rhetoric*, especially the passage (1389a–1390b) where he contrasts the idealism
and impulsiveness of youth with the caution and selfishness of
old age. Theophrastus (who was also a prolific writer on
scientific and philosophical subjects) had taken over the School
of Philosophy in Athens when Aristotle had retired in 323, and
Menander was one of his pupils. A dramatist would be well
advised to study the *Characters*, especially to perfect his dialogue. Theophrastus knows just how to bring to life his
Feckless or his Tiresome Man by the words he puts into their
mouths, and part of the charm of these witty sketches is that
their author knows exactly when to stop. Menander's own
skill in characteristic dialogue is apparent even from the few
fragments left of his plays.

*See *Menander: Plays and Fragments, and Theophrastus: The
Characters*, tr. Philip Vellacott (Penguin Classics, 1967).

Four of Terence's six plays were modelled on Menander's, two (*Phormio* and *The Mother-in-Law*) on plays by Apollodorus of Carystus. Plautus, the master of *vis comica* and creator of *opéra bouffe*, seems to have found Menander less to his taste; only three out of his twenty-one extant plays can be certainly said to have followed Menander. There is no simple answer to the question of how much in a play by Terence is original and how much directly due to the Greek model. Opinions range widely, from that of T. B. L. Webster, whose *Studies in Menander* quote Terence as evidence for the contents of the lost plays, to that of Gilbert Norwood in *The Art of Terence*, who is unwilling to allow anything to Menander at all. None of the plays Terence mentions in his prologues has survived, and the only complete play of Menander's we have (*Dyskolos, The Bad-Tempered Man*) is an early work which is lively and amusing but hardly subtle enough to justify Menander's immense reputation as long as his plays were there to be read and performed. But the larger surviving fragments of plays like *The Arbitration*, *The Unkindest Cut* and *The Samian Woman* are sufficient to show that Menander was a master of plot and dialogue, and a creator of characters who are more than types. Demeas, for instance, in *The Samian Woman*, is much more than a conventionally irritable husband and father, and Onesimus, the slave in *The Arbitration*, is something of a personality, rather like Syrus in Terence's *The Brothers*. Terence's well-loved tolerance and humanism are also a characteristic of Menander, who is equally quotable; their observations on life and its problems may not be strikingly original but they will always give pleasure because they ring true.

It is certain that Terence was never a *translator* of Greek plays. He does not mince his words about people who were – see, especially, the prologue to *The Eunuch*. Moreover, Donatus says explicitly in more than one of his commentaries that he had read the Greek originals, and in the case of *The Girl from Andros* he had studied closely both the plays cited in the prologue in order to estimate how Terence had used them. Sometimes he quotes a line in Greek to show that Terence took it over word-for-word, but the very fact that he singles out these passages for quotation shows that they were comparatively rare. Elsewhere he sometimes makes a point of remarking where Terence has improved on his original – the opening scene, in dialogue, of *The Girl from Andros*, or the re-modelling of the later part of *The Mother-in-Law*. There are, of course, some scenes in the extant portions of Menander which are very close to Terence; the episode between Pamphilus and Philumena described by Bacchis in *The Mother-in-Law* is very like the one discussed by Onesimus and Habrotonon in Menander's *The Arbitration*. This is to be expected, as the possible situations in comedy of this kind are relatively few and stereotyped, providing a recognized framework within which wit can sparkle and intrigue unfold. It is not really important for Terence's purposes what scene he selected from which play of Menander's, and this is what, with some impatience, he tries to tell his critics in the prologues. What matters is the artistic unity of the result. The world of High Comedy must always be artificial, and by definition limited, and this probably accounts for its relative unpopularity today.

Twenty years and more before Terence's time, Plautus had been a popular success with his 'Greek plays', and before him Ennius and Naevius had worked in the same way. All three are cited by Terence as dramatists he admired in the first, and most significant, of his prologues (*The Girl from Andros*). They had made free use of anything they liked in their models and had disregarded scenes in which they were not interested: this was their 'carelessness' (*neglegentia*). (The same word is used to describe Plautus' handling of a play in the Prologue to *The Brothers*.) It is contrasted with the 'dreary pedantry' (*obscura diligentia*) of their less talented imitators, notably the 'malevolent old playwright' Luscius Lanuvinus who, we may imagine, had offered the public a closer imitation of Greek models but 'for all his clever translation' had only succeeded in turning good Greek plays into bad Latin ones (Prologue to *The Eunuch*). Terence makes it quite clear that in his opinion Plautus' free use of the Greek plays was artistically justified.

One can feel a sneaking sympathy for Luscius Lanuvinus, plodding away at his translating, soured by his failures and infuriated by the successes of a young man half his age, not even a Roman nor free-born, the spoilt favourite of the influential Scipios,* as articulate as he is self-assured. That sudden leap to fame is suspicious – and where did the boy learn his Latin? Probably the Scipio set wrote the plays for him. Who is he, to mess about with all those Greek plays? If he picks over so many, there'll be none left for an honest translator. Nothing happens in his plays anyway – it's all talk, talk, not a bit of excitement, not even a dog allowed on the stage. Here's one supposed to be Menander's *Eunuch*, but he's not getting away with *that* – a lot of it's cribbed from Plautus' *Flatterer*. The undercurrent of carping criticism is audible through the prologues' sharp retorts.

Terence is proud of having the patronage of 'noble friends', but denies that they helped him with his plays. He dismisses the charge as a 'spiteful accusation' (*The Self-Tormentor* and *The Brothers*). He answers the charge of plagiarism by pointing out that he has only made use of stock situations and characters and ignored the plays of his Roman predecessors. He has no

* See the Introduction to *The Brothers*, p. 9.

intention of courting popularity by noisy crowd-scenes or animals on the stage (*Phormio* and *The Self-Tormentor*); all he asks for is an attentive audience. And if 'spoiling' plays (*contaminare*) means selecting what he wants from any source he likes, that is precisely what the great Plautus did and what Terence proposes to do.

A great deal has been said about the vexed question of *contaminatio*.* The normal meaning of the word is 'pollute' or 'soil', and in its specialized sense it appears twice in Terence and nowhere else. Luscius Lanuvinus in the Prologue to *The Girl from Andros* is quoted as protesting that this upstart young dramatist is 'soiling' or 'spoiling' Greek plays. In *The Self-Tormentor* he returns to the charge: Terence is 'spoiling' Greek plays for others by using more than one to make a single Latin play. It seems very unlikely that so strong a word could also mean no more than 'combine' (the traditional translation of these two passages). Luscius Lanuvinus surely means that Terence is making a Greek play useless to a straight translator if he picks bits out to incorporate in another play. Terence's answer is that he is determined to revert to the freedom of the earlier dramatists, seeing that pedantic accuracy in translation can never create a living Roman play.

The portrait of Terence himself which emerges from the prologues is one of a conscious artist, impatient of criticism which he feels to be malicious, and confident (as gifted young men must always be) that he has it in him to do good work. He is self-assured and intolerant of the second-rate, but he is as sensitive and eager for appreciation as one of his own young men. More than once he declares that his main concern is to give pleasure, and he knows very well that a play can never

*See W. Beare, *The Roman Stage*, third edn., App. K, and *Classical Review*, 1959; also W. R. Chalmers, *Classical Review*, 1957.

come to life without the support of its audience. Hence his repeated pleas for a fair hearing, if a young man is to make his way in the world, and the tone of hurt surprise in references to the repeated failure of *The Mother-in-Law*. (No doubt he was well aware that it was in many ways his best-constructed play.) He certainly thought that he was bringing something new to the stage, and I think we must allow that he did do this.

His chief original contribution was the double plot, for which so conscious an artist had his reasons: it enabled him to enlarge on his major interest, the effect of plot on character and the contrasted reactions of different kinds of character to the same situation. He could then draw carefully diversified portraits of closely connected persons, the two young men and the two old fathers in *The Brothers*, the two neighbours in *The Self-Tormentor*, the three young men in *The Eunuch*. He wrote Latin which is a joy to read, lucid and unadorned, the perfect counterpart of the Greek of Menander. He settled comedy firmly in the world of real life by removing the formal, expository prologue (which Plautus kept) and dispensing with divine intervention, thus making his plays both more theatrically effective and non-fantastical. He also went further than Menander (as far as we can judge from the fragments) in creating characters in the round, such as Phormio or Micio. He was more sympathetic towards old people – the father is never a mere dupe nor the mother a figure of fun – and more interested in women as persons; *The Mother-in-Law* is essentially a woman's play. The courtesan Bacchis has no counterpart in literature, though, oddly enough, according to Livy there was a fairly close parallel in history just before Terence was born. Hispala Fecenna, the courtesan freed-woman who gave evidence at the inquiry into the Bacchanalian orgies in Rome in 189 B.C., had been genuinely in love with her young neighbour Aebutius, had supported him in the face of opposition from his family, and made him her heir (Livy, XXXIX. 9–18). It is tempting to speculate whether Terence would have broken completely with the convention that plays must always be adapted from the Greek had he lived longer.

The three plays in this volume illustrate different sides of Terence's versatile talent; *The Girl from Andros* is romantic, *Phormio* pure comedy of intrigue, *The Self-Tormentor* an elaborate study of a complex plot and its effect on contrasted characters. As in the earlier volume, the translation follows the Oxford text of Kauer and Lindsay (revised 1958), with help from the French Budé text of J. Marouzeau, the commentaries of Donatus and Eugraphius, and the special editions listed in the Bibliography. No attempt has been made to reproduce Terence's verse because of the 'traditional association between the comic genre and the prose form'.*

Philip Vellacott's work on Menander and Theophrastus has made it possible for readers of this series of translations to look at Terence as an inheritor of classic comedy's conventions as well as the chief medium through which they passed to the post-Renaissance stage. Once more E. F. Watling's keen stage sense and practical experience have come to my aid when commentaries failed to enlighten, and I am grateful for his generous help.

B.R.

Highgate, 1966

* See George Steiner, *The Death of Tragedy* (1961), pp. 247 ff.

THE GIRL FROM ANDROS

[ANDRIA]

INTRODUCTORY NOTE

IT is generally agreed that *The Girl from Andros* is Terence's first play and was performed in 166 B.C., when the author was twenty-one. The Prologue is aimed at answering his critics, so either it was written for a later performance, or the play must have been known to his rivals even earlier (perhaps at a rehearsal similar to the one described in the Author's Prologue to *The Eunuch*). Terence's sympathetic treatment of the conventional theme of a young man in love with a girl he cannot legally marry makes this the first truly romantic comedy, and the first scene has been admired and quoted by critics from Cicero onwards. The commentator Donatus also says explicitly that Terence replaced a less dramatic monologue in the opening scene of Menander's *The Girl from Samos* by the conversation between Simo and his freedman as we have it, taking the idea from *The Girl from Perinthos*.

The alternative ending may have been an acting variation on Terence's original or a literary effort on the part of someone dissatisfied with what at first sight seems rather an abrupt settlement of the fortunes of the second young couple, Charinus and Philumena; but Terence is surely dramatically right in refusing to repeat a betrothal scene on-stage, and he solves the problem neatly by Davos' final words. This is, moreover, his practice elsewhere – in *The Self-Tormentor* Clinia disappears from the scene some time before the end of the play, so that interest can be concentrated on Clitipho.

The Prologue makes it clear that the double plot is also Terence's innovation, and he is thus enabled to draw the contrast between the two young men, the histrionic Charinus and

Pamphilus, who is more fully realized as an ardently romantic young man, with something of his father Simo's forceful character. This is one of Terence's liveliest plays, allowing full scope for the ingenuity of the resourceful Davos.

PRODUCTION NOTICE

(A paraphrase supplied by Donatus; the original is missing from the MSS.)

This is the author's first play, performed at the Megalesian Games★ during the curule aedileship of Marcus Fulvius, Manius Glabrio and Quintus Minucius Valerius.

Produced by Lucius Atilius of Praeneste and Lucius Ambivius Turpio. Music composed by Flaccus, son (*for* slave) of Claudius, for matched pipes, either right or left hand.†

Greek original followed throughout.

Composed during the consulship of Marcus Marcellus and Gaius Sulpicius.‡

  ★Celebrated annually on 4 April in honour of the Great Mother, the goddess Cybele.
  †Meaning obscure.
  ‡i.e. 166 B.C.

SYNOPSIS*

Glycerium, who is wrongly supposed to be the sister of a courtesan from Andros, is seduced and made pregnant by Pamphilus. He then promises to marry her, but his father, Simo, has already arranged another marriage for him with the daughter of Chremes. On hearing of Pamphilus' affair Simo pretends that the other wedding will still take place, hoping thereby to discover his son's real feelings. On the advice of his slave Davos Pamphilus raises no objections, but when Glycerium's child is born and Chremes sees it, he breaks off the marriage with Pamphilus. Afterwards, he discovers to his surprise that Glycerium is really his daughter, so he marries her to Pamphilus and his other daughter to Charinus.

* All Terence's plays have a synopsis written in the mid second century A.D. by Gaius Sulpicius Apollinaris of Carthage.

AUTHOR'S PROLOGUE TO
THE GIRL FROM ANDROS

When the author first turned his thoughts to writing, he supposed that his sole concern was to write plays which would give pleasure to his audience. He has since learned how different things are in practice; for he now spends his time writing prologues, not to explain the plot of a play but to answer the slanderous attacks of a malevolent old playwright.*

Now please note the charge he faces today. Menander wrote two plays, *The Girl from Andros* and *The Girl from Perinthos*; know one and you know them both, for the plots are much the same, though there are differences in dialogue and style. The author admits that he has made free use of anything suitable from the latter play and transferred it to his adaptation of the former. This is the practice attacked by his critics, who argue that by so doing he is 'spoiling'† the original plays. Surely they miss the point here, for all their cleverness. In attacking the present author they are really attacking his models, Naevius, Plautus and Ennius, whose 'carelessness' he would far rather imitate than his critics' dreary pedantry. He therefore bids them hold their peace in future, and stop making these insinuations; or else they may find their own failings exposed.

Now pay attention, give us your support and a fair hearing; then you may determine what hope there is for the future – whether the author's coming plays will merit a showing or deserve to be driven off the stage unheard.

*Luscius Lanuvinus, Terence's rival and critic.
†See Introduction, p. 12.

CHARACTERS

SIMO	*an Athenian gentleman*
SOSIA	*his elderly freedman*
PAMPHILUS	*his son, in love with Glycerium*
CHREMES	*a neighbour*
CHARINUS	*a friend of Pamphilus, in love with Chremes'* *daughter Philumena*
CRITO	*a visitor from Andros, cousin to Chrysis*
DAVOS	*a slave of Simo, attendant on Pamphilus*
DROMO	*a slave of Simo*
BYRRIA	*a slave of Charinus*
MYSIS	*a maidservant of Glycerium*
LESBIA	*a midwife*
CANTHARA	*her assistant*

(Chrysis, a courtesan from Andros, has died before the play opens. Glycerium, 'the girl from Andros', and Chremes' daughter Philumena do not appear)

*

The scene is laid in Athens in front of the houses of Simo and Glycerium. To the audience's right the street leads to the centre of the town, to their left to the harbour and the house of Chremes

[SIMO, *a gentleman in late middle age, and his elderly freed slave* SOSIA *come on right with servants carrying food and drink for a party*.]

SIMO: Take those things in, boys; hurry up. Sosia, wait a minute, I want a word with you.

[*The servants go into his house*.]

SOSIA: No need to tell me, sir. I expect you want me to take charge of all that.

SIMO: No, it's something else.

SOSIA: But what better use can you make of my services?

SIMO: I don't need your professional skill at the moment; this demands the qualities I have always observed in you – loyalty and secrecy.

SOSIA: I'm at your service, sir.

SIMO: You know that ever since I bought you for my slave as a boy you have found me a just and considerate master. I gave you your freedom because you served me in a free spirit, and that was the highest reward at my disposal.

SOSIA: I don't forget it, sir.

SIMO: And I don't regret it.

SOSIA: I'm only too glad if anything I've said or done pleases you, sir, and I'm grateful for your gracious approval. But I'm a bit worried about the way you're reminding me about the circumstances – it looks like a reproach for ingratitude. Please tell me briefly what you want of me.

SIMO: I will. Let me start by saying that you're wrong about these preparations. There isn't really going to be a wedding.

SOSIA: Then why pretend there is?

SIMO: I'll tell you the whole story, then you'll know all about my son's conduct, my own plans and the part I want you to play in the matter. As soon as Pamphilus was grown up and had more freedom – for no one could have known the truth or guessed his disposition as long as he was restrained by youth, timidity and his tutor –

SOSIA: That's true.

SIMO: The usual things young men do, their crazes for keeping horses or hounds or dabbling in philosophy, all took up his time to a certain extent, but he hadn't any special enthusiasms. I was pleased.

SOSIA: And rightly, sir. 'Nothing too much' is the best rule in life.

SIMO: Let me tell you the sort of life he lived: he was patient and tolerant with all his friends, fell in with the wishes of any of them and joined in all their pursuits, never contradicting nor putting himself first. That's the best way to steer clear of jealousy, win a reputation and make friends.

SOSIA: A well-planned life! Agree with everything nowadays, if you want friends; truthfulness doesn't pay.

SIMO: Meanwhile a woman came from Andros three years ago and settled down in the neighbourhood, the victim of poverty and the indifference of her relatives: a beautiful girl, in the flower of her youth.

SOSIA: Aha; I suspect she brings trouble with her.

SIMO: At first she led a modest life, thrifty and hard-working, trying to make a living out of spinning and weaving. Then lovers began to come, first one and then another; human nature takes to pleasure all too easily after a spell of hard labour, and so she accepted their offers and soon afterwards set up as a professional. One day her current lovers happened to take my son there to dinner. 'Now he's caught,' I said to myself at once; 'she's got him.' I used to watch his friends'

servant-boys coming and going every morning and call to
them: 'You there! Can you tell me who was in favour with
Chrysis yesterday?' (That was the woman's name.)

SOSIA: I see.

SIMO: They said it was Phaedrus or Clinias or Niceratus, for
these three shared her at the time. 'What about Pamphilus?'
'Oh, he only stayed to dinner and paid his share.' I was delighted. I made the same inquiry another day, and found
nothing at all to implicate Pamphilus. Naturally I concluded
that he was a model of continence, tried and tested, for if a
man's will has come up against characters like theirs and
remained unmoved you may feel sure of his self-control in
his own way of life. To add to my satisfaction, everyone
spoke well of him with one voice and congratulated me on
my good fortune in having a son blessed with such character.
Well, to cut a long story short, my neighbour Chremes was
persuaded by what he'd heard to approach me of his own
accord and offer his only daughter with a substantial dowry
to my son in marriage. I approved and accepted the match,
and today is the day fixed for the wedding.

SOSIA: What's stopping it then?

SIMO: You'll hear. A few days after we made the agreement
our neighbour Chrysis died.

SOSIA: Good, I'm glad to hear it. She made me nervous for
Pamphilus.

SIMO: At the time my son was always at the house with Chrysis' lovers, helping them with the funeral. He was often
depressed and sometimes in tears. I was quite pleased at the
time, for if he took this woman's death so much to heart, I
thought, when they were only slightly acquainted, what
would he feel if he had been really in love? And how will he
take it when death comes to me, his father? I assumed that

everything was prompted by his sensitive nature and sympathetic disposition. In short, I went to the funeral myself to please him, still with no suspicion that anything was wrong.

SOSIA: What are you getting at, sir?

SIMO: I'll tell you. The body was brought out and we followed. Presently among the women there I caught sight of a young girl whose beauty was –

SOSIA: Not bad, perhaps.

SIMO: And her expression, Sosia, was so modest and lovely – nothing could be more so. Her grief seemed to me to exceed that of the other women, just as she outshone them all in the grace and refinement of her bearing, so I went up to the attendants and asked them who she was. They told me she was the sister of Chrysis. Then the truth came home to me. Why, that was it – the reason for his tears and tenderheartedness.

SOSIA: I dread to think what's coming next!

SIMO: Meanwhile the procession moved off, we joined it and came to the cemetery. The body was laid on the pyre. Everyone wept. Then the sister I spoke of, careless of what she did, went dangerously near the flames. Thereupon Pamphilus, in his terror, let out the secret of his well-hidden love. He ran up and caught her round the waist. 'Glycerium, my darling,' he cried, 'what are you doing? You'll kill yourself.' Then you could easily see that they had long been lovers; she fell back into his arms and wept, so confidingly . . .

SOSIA: Did she indeed!

SIMO: I returned home angry and disappointed in him, but I had no real grounds for reproving him. I could imagine his answer: 'What have I done, father? What's wrong? A girl tried to throw herself on the fire, and I held her back and saved her life. There's no harm in that.' Plausible enough.

SOSIA: You're right, sir. If you start blaming folk for saving lives, what will you do with those who do real harm or damage?

SIMO: Next day Chremes came to me full of complaints at what he'd discovered: Pamphilus regarded this foreigner as his wife – a shocking affair! I hotly denied it. He insisted it was true. When we eventually parted he made it quite clear that he was withdrawing his consent to his daughter's marriage.

SOSIA: And your son, sir? Didn't you –

SIMO: No. I still hadn't good enough grounds for reproving him.

SOSIA: Why? Please explain.

SIMO: Again, he'd have his answer: 'You've named the date for this to stop yourself, father. I shall have to adapt myself to another person's ways soon enough; meanwhile you might let me live my own life.'

SOSIA: Then how can you get at him?

SIMO: Well, he may refuse to marry at all on account of this love-affair; that would be a real act of insolence, and I couldn't let it pass. I'm now trying to find a genuine reason for rebuking him by this pretence of wedding preparations, to see if he refuses to take part. At the same time, if that scoundrel Davos has some trap in hand I hope to make him spring it now while his tricks can do no harm. I fancy he'll fight tooth and nail for anything he's set on, and more to annoy me than to please my son.

SOSIA: Why, sir?

SIMO: Oh, you know: evil nature, evil mind. If I catch him – Well, that'll do. But if it turns out as I'd like and Pamphilus makes no difficulties, then I've only got Chremes to talk over, and I've hopes of succeeding there. Now it's your job for the moment to make a good show of this wedding, intimidate Davos, keep an eye on my son's doings and see if the two of them are plotting anything.

SOSIA: Right, sir. I'll see to that.

SIMO: Let's go in then. You go ahead, I'll follow.

[SOSIA *goes into* SIMO'S *house, but* SIMO *is prevented by the arrival of his smart young servant,* DAVOS.]

I feel pretty sure that Pamphilus *will* refuse, for I could see before that Davos was alarmed when he heard there was to be a wedding. But here he comes.

[DAVOS *comes on right.*]

DAVOS: I always was surprised that we could get away with it like that – I'd doubts all along about the way the master took the news so calmly. From the moment he heard his son's engagement was off he's never said a word to any of us and didn't appear to be at all annoyed.

SIMO [*aside*]: But he'll say one now – as you'll know to your cost.

DAVOS: Maybe he intended to lead us on with false rejoicing, off our guard as we were, full of hope, suspecting nothing, and then catch us unawares before we'd a chance to put a stop to the wedding: the artful beggar!

SIMO: What's the rascal saying?

DAVOS: It's the master! I didn't see him.

SIMO: Davos!

DAVOS: What is it, sir?

SIMO: Turn round and look at me.

DAVOS [*not doing so*]: *Now* what does he want?

SIMO: Look here –

DAVOS: What at?

SIMO: Don't be silly. [DAVOS *reluctantly faces him*.] There's gossip – that my son's having an affair.

DAVOS [*cynically*]: Oh yes, the public's very interested; of course.

SIMO: Are you listening to me?

DAVOS: Of course I am.

SIMO: I don't intend to go into that any further. I'm not an unreasonable parent, and his past conduct is none of my concern. As long as circumstances permitted I left him free to do as he liked, but today must mark the beginning of a new life and demands a change in his ways. Consequently, I'm telling you, and I might even go so far as to beg you, Davos, to lead him back to the right path. Let me explain. Any man with a mistress dislikes having to take a wife –

DAVOS: So they say.

SIMO: Then if he comes under a bad influence concerning these matters, it directs his mind, lovesick as it is, towards the worse decision.

DAVOS: Sorry, sir, I can't understand a word you're saying.

SIMO: Nonsense!

DAVOS: I'm no good at riddles, sir; my name's Davos, not Oedipus.

SIMO: Then I suppose you prefer plain words? I haven't finished yet.

DAVOS: Yes, please, sir.

SIMO: If I catch you up to any of your tricks today to prevent this marriage or trying to show off your cleverness, I warn you, Davos, I'll have you beaten senseless and sent to the mill, with my solemn assurance that if I let you out I shall go there and grind in your place. Is that quite clear? Or is there something you still can't understand?

DAVOS: I understand all right, sir. You spoke nice and plain
this time, no roundabout way at all.

SIMO: This is the one thing where I simply will not be put off
by any of your swindles.

DAVOS: Hush, hush, sir.

SIMO: You're laughing at me, I can see. But I'm telling you
this, Davos: don't do anything rash, and don't say you
haven't been warned. Be careful.

[*He goes off, right.*]

DAVOS: Well, Davos, if the old man meant all he was saying
just now about a wedding, this is no time for slackness and
go-slow methods. I must look out *and* look sharp or it'll be
the death of me and my young master. I'm not quite sure
what to do, help Pamphilus or listen to *him*. If I abandon
Pamphilus I'm afraid for his life, and if I help him there's the
old chap's threats, and he's not easy to deceive. In the first
place he's found out about the affair, and he's watching me
like the menace he is to see I don't trick him over the wedding. If he finds me out, I'm finished; or if the whim takes
him, he'll find a reason, right or wrong, to pack me off to
the mill. And there's another problem: this girl from
Andros, whether she's wife or mistress, is having a baby,
and Pamphilus is the father. You ought to hear their crazy
plans – they act more like lunatics than lovers. They're
determined to acknowledge the child, boy or girl, and now
they're concocting a silly story that the mother is Athenian
born. There was a man once, they say, a merchant who was
shipwrecked off Andros and lost his life. His orphaned child
was washed ashore and Chrysis' father took her in. Nonsense I call it, a most unlikely tale, but they're pleased with
their fabrication. [*The door of* GLYCERIUM's *house opens and
her servant,* MYSIS, *comes out.*] Now here's Mysis coming out

of her mistress's house. I'll slip off into town and find Pamphilus. I don't want his father to spring this on him unawares.

[*He goes off, right.*]

MYSIS [*talking to the housekeeper indoors*]: All right, Archylis, I heard you long ago; you want Lesbia fetched. I tell you, the woman drinks and she's careless, quite unsuitable in fact to be entrusted with a first confinement. Shall I fetch her all the same? [*To the audience*] Look at the obstinacy of the old fool – all because the two of them take their drinks together! I pray heaven that my mistress will have an easy labour and the midwife won't do one of her bungled jobs here – others can have them. [*Looking right down the street*] Why, I do believe that's Pamphilus, and what a state he's in! I'm afraid something's wrong. I'll just wait to see if this means trouble for us.

[PAMPHILUS *rushes on, in a state of agitation; evidently he has missed* DAVOS *but seen his father.*]

PAMPHILUS [*not seeing* MYSIS]: Oh, what a thing to do! The very idea! It's inhuman. Is this what you expect from a father?

MYSIS: Whatever's this?

PAMPHILUS: My God, if this isn't an outrage, what is? He'd made up his mind to marry me off today. Shouldn't I have had notice? Couldn't he have told me before?

MYSIS: Mercy me, what's this I hear!

PAMPHILUS: And what about Chremes? He'd refused once to trust me with his daughter; has he changed his mind – because he sees I haven't changed mine? Is he absolutely set on tearing me away from Glycerium and ruining my happiness? If he succeeds . . . it'll kill me. Oh, is any man so crossed in love and cursed by fortune as I am! Heaven and earth, can't there be some way of escape from Chremes and this marriage? See how I'm mocked and scorned – and now everything's fixed and settled – how I'm refused and then recalled – what's the reason for it? Maybe my suspicions are right and they're harbouring a freak whom they can't palm off on anyone else – so they pick on me.

MYSIS: Oh dear, dear, I'm really frightened.

PAMPHILUS: As for my father, words fail me. How *could* he treat something so serious in this off-hand way? He passed me in the street just now. 'You're to be married today, Pamphilus,' was all he said: 'go home at once and get ready.' To me it sounded like 'Clear off and hang yourself.' I was staggered, couldn't get a word out, or any excuse, however false or silly or inept – struck dumb in fact. If I'd known of it before and anyone asked me now what I'd do – I'd do *something*, if only not to be doing this. . . . As it is, what can I set about first? So many worries block my path, pull me opposite ways: my love and pity for Glycerium, anxiety over this wedding, respect for my father who has been so indulgent up till now and let me do anything I liked. How can I think of going against him? Oh, it's terrible! What can I do? I just don't know.

MYSIS: That sounds bad; I don't like the sound of 'don't know' at all. But the main thing now is for him to talk to my mistress or for me to have a word with him about her. It doesn't take much to tip the balance either way when a man's in two minds.

PAMPHILUS [*waking up to her presence*]: Who's that talking? Oh, hullo, Mysis.

MYSIS: Good morning, sir.

PAMPHILUS: How are things going?

MYSIS: You should know. She's racked with labour pains,

poor soul, and torn by anxiety when she remembers that this was the day fixed for your wedding. She's terrified too that you'll abandon her.

PAMPHILUS [*indignantly*]: How could I think of doing such a thing? Shall I let this poor girl be deceived on my account, after she had trusted me with her heart, nay, her very life, and I had treated her as the darling of my heart with all a husband's devotion? She was formed and fashioned in purity and virtue; should I allow her whole character to be changed through pressure of poverty? Of course not!

MYSIS: I shouldn't worry if it all rested with you, sir, but suppose they use force – can you stand up to it?

PAMPHILUS: Do you really think me so spiritless and unfeeling, so cruel and unnatural? Could I remain unmoved when thoughts of our love and association and my sense of honour all prompt me to keep my word?

MYSIS: One thing I do know, sir; she has earned the right to be remembered by you.

PAMPHILUS: *Remembered?* Oh, Mysis, Mysis, the words Chrysis used of her are forever written in my heart. Almost with her last breath she called me to her side; I drew near, and you all withdrew; we were alone. Then she began: 'My dear Pamphilus, you see this girl's youth and beauty, and you are well aware how little use these are to her today to protect her honour and property. Wherefore, by this right hand and your own better self, in the name of your pledged word and her own lonely state, I implore you not to put her from you nor abandon her. As surely as I have loved you like my own brother, and she has set you above all others and sought to please you in everything, I give you to her as husband and friend, guardian and parent; I bequeath you all our property here, and entrust it to your safe-keeping.'

So she gave Glycerium into my care, and death took her at once. I accepted the charge; it is one I shall not lay down.

MYSIS: I hope not, sir.

[*She starts to go.*]

PAMPHILUS: Why are you leaving her now?

MYSIS: I'm fetching the midwife.

PAMPHILUS: Be quick then, and listen – not a word about this wedding. In her present condition –

MYSIS: I understand.

[*She goes off right, and* PAMPHILUS *moves to the other side of the stage, absorbed in his troubles, so that he does not notice the entry, right, of his friend* CHARINUS, *accompanied by his servant,* BYRRIA.]

CHARINUS: What's that, Byrria? Did you say Philumena was to be married to Pamphilus today?

BYRRIA: That's right.

CHARINUS: How do you know?

BYRRIA: I met Davos in town just now, and he told me.

CHARINUS: Oh, it's terrible! Up to now I've been torn between hope and fear – now all hope's lost and I'm left with a mind numbed by anxiety, worn out and exhausted.

BYRRIA: Good heavens, sir, if you can't have what you want, do try to want what you can have.

CHARINUS [*despondently*]: I don't want anything but Philumena.

BYRRIA: You'd do far better to make an effort to rid yourself of this passion, instead of saying things which only add fuel to the fire and do no good.

CHARINUS: It's easy for any healthy person to give good advice to a sick man. If you were in my place you'd think differently.

BYRRIA: All right, have it your own way.

CHARINUS: Look, there's Pamphilus. I must try everything before I accept defeat.

BYRRIA [*aside*]: What's he up to?

CHARINUS: I'll appeal to him in person, fall at his knees, tell him of my love – I believe that'll persuade him at least to postpone the wedding for a few days. Meanwhile something'll turn up – I hope.

BYRRIA [*aside*]: 'Something'? Nothing, more like.

CHARINUS: What do you think, Byrria; shall I go up to him?

BYRRIA: You might as well; at least you'll succeed in giving him the idea that you're all set to be his wife's lover, if he marries her.

CHARINUS: Oh go to hell, you and your insinuations, you rascal!

PAMPHILUS [*waking up to their presence*]: Why, here's Charinus. Hullo.

CHARINUS: Hullo, Pamphilus. I come to you in search of hope, salvation, aid and counsel.

PAMPHILUS: I'm in no position to give advice, and I've no means of helping you. But what's the matter?

CHARINUS: Are you getting married today?

PAMPHILUS: So they say.

CHARINUS [*dramatically*]: Pamphilus, if you do so, this is the last time you will set eyes on me.

PAMPHILUS [*genuinely surprised*]: Why on earth?

CHARINUS: Alas, I dare not say. Byrria, you tell him.

BYRRIA: All right.

PAMPHILUS: Then what is it?

BYRRIA: He's in love – with the girl you're to marry.

PAMPHILUS: Which is more than I am . . . . [*Hopefully*] Now tell me, Charinus, has there been anything more between you?

CHARINUS: No, Pamphilus, nothing at all.

PAMPHILUS: If only there had!

CHARINUS: In the name of our friendship and my love for Philumena, I beseech you: don't marry her. That would be best.

PAMPHILUS: I'll certainly *try* not to.

CHARINUS: But if that proves impossible, or your heart is set on this marriage –

PAMPHILUS: *Set* on it!

CHARINUS: – do at least postpone it for a few days so that I can go away and not see it.

PAMPHILUS: Now let me speak, Charinus. I don't want credit when none is deserved. I don't think any gentleman should expect it. And in the case of this marriage – I'm much more anxious to get out of it than you are to take it on.

CHARINUS: Oh, I can breathe again!

PAMPHILUS: Now you and Byrria here do all you can, plot and plan and devise some means of getting the girl for yourself. On my side I'll do my best not to have her.

CHARINUS: I'm willing.

PAMPHILUS [*looking along the street*]: Splendid, I can see Davos. He always has some good suggestions.

CHARINUS [*to* BYRRIA]: While yours, damn you, if you have any, are quite useless. You can go.

BYRRIA [*rudely*]: That suits me!

[*He goes off left as* DAVOS *hurries on right, too excited to see the young men.*]

DAVOS: Good heavens, good news! Now where's Pamphilus? I'll set his mind at rest and fill his heart with joy!

CHARINUS [*dubiously*]: Something's made him happy.

PAMPHILUS: Nothing in it. He hasn't heard our present troubles.

DAVOS [*still to himself*]: If he's heard by now there's a wedding prepared for him I expect he's –

CHARINUS: There, did you hear that?

DAVOS: – hunting wildly for me all over the town. Where can he be? Where shall I look first?

CHARINUS: Quick, speak to him.

DAVOS [*beginning to move off*]: I know –

PAMPHILUS: Davos, here, stop!

DAVOS: Who's that? Oh sir, the very man I want! And Charinus, hurrah! The two of you, how splendid! I need you both.

PAMPHILUS: Davos, I'm lost.

DAVOS: Just you listen to this –

CHARINUS: I'm finished.

DAVOS [*to* CHARINUS]: I know what you're afraid of.

PAMPHILUS: My life hangs in the balance.

DAVOS [*to* PAMPHILUS]: And you too: I know.

PAMPHILUS: That wedding for me –

DAVOS: I know.

PAMPHILUS: – today –

DAVOS: Why go on and on when I keep telling you I *know*? [*To* PAMPHILUS] You're afraid you'll have to marry the girl. [*To* CHARINUS] And you're afraid you can't.

CHARINUS: You've got it.

PAMPHILUS: Absolutely.

DAVOS: And there's absolutely no danger. Trust me.

PAMPHILUS: I implore you, free me quickly from my wretched fears.

DAVOS: All right, I'm freeing you now. Chremes has withdrawn his offer.

PAMPHILUS: How do you know?

DAVOS: I know all right. Your father stopped me just now,

told me you were to be married today, and a whole lot more things I haven't time to repeat now. I ran off at once to tell you. When I couldn't find you anywhere I climbed up a hill and looked all round – no sign of you. Then I caught sight of your man Byrria [*addressing* CHARINUS] and asked him. He said he hadn't seen you. I was worried and wondered what to do. On my way back I had a sudden suspicion: 'Why, there was very little bought for dinner, the master was in a bad temper, and the wedding was all very sudden: it doesn't make sense.'

PAMPHILUS: What are you getting at?

DAVOS: I went straight along to Chremes'. Not a soul outside the house when I got there. I was delighted.

CHARINUS [*eagerly*]: You're right.

PAMPHILUS: Go on.

DAVOS: I waited. During this time I saw no one go in, no one come out. There were no married women about the house, no preparations, no excitement. I went up and peeped in –

PAMPHILUS: I see. That's good proof.

DAVOS [*triumphantly*]: Does this look like a wedding?

PAMPHILUS: No, I don't think it does.

DAVOS: Only '*think*', sir? You can't have understood me. It's certain. What's more, as I came away I ran into Chremes' boy, and all he was carrying was a pennorth of greens and a few scraps of fish for the old man's supper.

CHARINUS: I'm saved too, Davos, thanks to you.

DAVOS: Indeed you're not!

CHARINUS: Why not? He isn't marrying her to *him* [*indicating* PAMPHILUS] after all.

DAVOS: Don't be so silly. It doesn't follow that *you*'ll marry her if Pamphilus doesn't. You'll have to take action, go round and canvass the old man's friends.

CHARINUS: You're right. I'll go, though heaven knows my hopes have come to nothing more often than not. Good-bye.

[*He goes off, left.*]

PAMPHILUS: What does my father mean by this play-acting?

DAVOS: I can tell you. If he shows annoyance now at Chremes' refusing to give you his daughter, before he finds out your attitude to the match, he thinks he'll put himself in the wrong – and rightly. But if you're the one who refuses to marry the girl, he can shift the blame on to you – and then there'll be the usual scene.

PAMPHILUS: I can face anything.

DAVOS: But he's your father, sir, that's the problem; and besides, your lady hasn't anyone to stand up for her. He'll find a pretext for throwing her out of the town, no sooner said than done.

PAMPHILUS [*horrified*]: Throwing her out?

DAVOS: In no time.

PAMPHILUS: Then tell me what I can do.

DAVOS: Agree to marry.

PAMPHILUS: What!

DAVOS: What's the matter?

PAMPHILUS: How can I do that?

DAVOS: Why not?

PAMPHILUS: I absolutely refuse.

DAVOS: I shouldn't do that, sir.

PAMPHILUS: I don't want any of your advice.

DAVOS: Think of the effect –

PAMPHILUS: I know. Cut off from *her* and shut up in *there* [*indicating* GLYCERIUM'*s and* SIMO'*s houses*].

DAVOS: No, no, you're wrong. What'll happen I'm sure is that your father will say he wants the wedding today. You'll say you're ready. He can't quarrel with that, and then you'll be able to upset all his well-laid plans without any risk to yourself, for it's quite certain that Chremes will refuse to give you his daughter. You needn't hold back for fear he'll change his mind. Tell your father you're willing so that he can't be angry with you, whatever he wants. You may hope it'll be easy to fend off a wife – 'with a character like mine no one will give me one' is what you'll say, but he's more likely to produce a penniless bride for you than leave you to go to the bad. But if he finds you raise no objection he'll worry much less and take his time to look for someone else for you. Meanwhile your luck may turn.

PAMPHILUS [*dubiously*]: Do you really think so?

DAVOS: I'm positive, sir.

PAMPHILUS: Think where you may land me.

DAVOS: Now, don't argue.

PAMPHILUS: All right, I'll agree. But he mustn't know about Glycerium's child, for I've promised to acknowledge it as mine.

DAVOS: *That* was rash!

PAMPHILUS: It was a promise she begged of me, to make sure I wouldn't abandon her.

DAVOS: We'll keep it. But here's your father. Take care he doesn't see you looking worried.

[SIMO *comes on right, not seeing the others as they draw back.*]

SIMO: I'm back to see what they're up to and what plans they've laid.

DAVOS [*to* PAMPHILUS]: You see he's quite certain you'll refuse to marry. He's been rehearsing his speech in some lonely spot and now he comes hoping it'll make mincemeat of you. Mind you keep your wits about you.

PAMPHILUS: I only hope I can!

DAVOS: Believe me, sir, just say you'll agree to take a wife and your father won't breathe another word.

[BYRRIA *comes on left, and stands unseen by the other three.*]

BYRRIA: Young Charinus told me to drop everything and spend the day watching Pamphilus, to find out his intentions about this marriage. That's why I'm trailing this one [*indicating* SIMO]. Why, there *is* Pamphilus with Davos – I'll stick to them [*moving nearer*].

SIMO [*turning to see* PAMPHILUS *and* DAVOS]: There they are, the pair of them.

DAVOS [*to* PAMPHILUS]: Now, remember!

SIMO: Pamphilus!

DAVOS: Turn round as if you hadn't seen him.

PAMPHILUS [*with marked surprise*]: Why, Father, is that you?

DAVOS [*aside*]: Well done!

SIMO [*watching him closely*]: Today, as I told you before, is the day on which I wish you to take a wife.

BYRRIA [*aside*]: What'll he answer? I'm nervous on our behalf.

PAMPHILUS [*sweetly*]: Neither in this nor in anything else will you meet with any opposition from me, Father.

BYRRIA: What!

DAVOS: He's struck dumb.

BYRRIA: What did he say?

SIMO [*somewhat nonplussed*]: It is very right and proper of you to accede to my request with a good grace.

DAVOS [*in triumph*]: There, was I right?

BYRRIA: It sounds as though my master's done out of a wife.

SIMO: Go indoors now, and don't keep us waiting when you're wanted.

PAMPHILUS: All right. [*He goes into* SIMO'*s house.*]

BYRRIA [*indignantly*]: Oh, you can't trust anyone in anything! It's quite true what you're always hearing, that no one thinks of anyone but himself. I've seen that girl, and I remember she was a real beauty, so I can understand if Pamphilus chose to have her sleeping in his own arms and not in my master's. . . . Well, I'll have to break the news – a blow for him and blows for me.

[*He goes off left, still unseen by the other two.*]

DAVOS [*aside*]: Now he thinks I've stayed behind because I've got a trick up my sleeve.

SIMO [*catching something of this*]: What's that you say?

DAVOS [*aloud*]: Nothing, same as before.

SIMO: Really?

DAVOS: Nothing at all.

SIMO [*aside*]: All the same I really thought –

DAVOS [*aside*]: He didn't expect this, I can see, and it's put him out of his stride.

SIMO: Are you capable of speaking the truth?

DAVOS: Of course, sir, that's easy.

SIMO: Doesn't my son find the prospect of marriage at all unwelcome on account of his association with this foreigner?

DAVOS: No, sir, not at all; or if he did, it would only worry him for two or three days, you know, and then he'd get over it. He's thought it all over properly in his own mind.

SIMO: Very creditable of him.

DAVOS: It was an affair of his youth, sir, which he only carried on as long as he could, and what's more, he kept it dark and took care his reputation shouldn't suffer, as a decent man should. Now it's time he took a wife, and he's got no thought for anything else.

SIMO: I thought he was looking a little bit depressed?

DAVOS: He may be a bit cross with you, sir, but that's another matter.

SIMO: What is it then?

DAVOS: Oh it's too silly –

SIMO: What *is* it?

DAVOS: Nothing, sir.

SIMO: What is it? Tell me at once.

DAVOS [*with a show of reluctance*]: He says you're, well, mean with your money.

SIMO: *I* am?

DAVOS: Yes, you, sir. 'Scarcely ten drachmas spent on the wedding-breakfast' is what he's saying. 'That doesn't look like a wedding for a son. I'll have to pick and choose among my friends if I'm to send out any invitations.' And if I may say so, sir, you really are terribly careful with your money. It isn't very creditable of you.

SIMO: Be quiet.

DAVOS [*aside*]: That stung him.

SIMO: I shall have this put right at once. [*Aside*] But there's something queer here. Is he up to his usual tricks? If it means mischief, you can be sure he's at the bottom of it.

[*They stand back as* MYSIS *returns, right, with* LESBIA, *the midwife, and her assistant,* CANTHARA.]

MYSIS: The fact is, Lesbia, as you said, there's scarcely a man to be found who'll stay faithful to a woman.

SIMO [*to* DAVOS]: It's the Andrian girl's servant.

DAVOS: What's that? So it is.

MYSIS: But Pamphilus –

SIMO: What!

MYSIS: – has confirmed our belief in him –

SIMO [*groans*]

DAVOS: If only he were deaf or she were dumb!

MYSIS: – by promising the child shall be acknowledged.

SIMO: My God, what do I hear? If what she says is true – it's the end.

LESBIA: He must be a really nice young gentleman.

MYSIS: He couldn't be better. But come in with me now, you mustn't keep my lady waiting.

LESBIA: After you.

[*They go into* GLYCERIUM's *house.*]

DAVOS [*aside*]: Now I've got to find a way out of *this* mess.

SIMO: Good heavens, how can he be so crazy? A foreign woman's child? [*After a pause*] Now I know! How slow I've been. At last I'm beginning to understand. . . .

DAVOS [*aside*]: *What* does he understand?

SIMO: This is the first stage of their plan to deceive me; the baby is all a pretence to frighten off Chremes.

GLYCERIUM [*calling from the house*]: Oh Juno Lucina, help me, save me, please!

SIMO [*whistling in surprise*]: As quick as that? It's absurd. She must have decided to speed up when she heard I was outside the door. There's something wrong with your timing, Davos.

DAVOS: Me, sir?

SIMO: Your pupils don't seem to know their parts.

DAVOS: I don't know what you mean, sir.

SIMO [*aside*]: If it had been a real marriage and this fellow had caught me unprepared, how he'd have had the laugh on me! As it is, he's the one in danger and my ship's in safe harbour.

[*The midwife comes out of the house, calling her instructions inside.*]

LESBIA: So far everything seems normal, Archylis, and she should be quite all right. First of all then, see that she has a bath; after that, give her the drink I ordered for her, just as much as I prescribed. [*Coming forward*] Bless me, that's a fine boy for Pamphilus! I pray heaven he'll live, for his

father's a real gentleman and wouldn't dream of wronging
such a nice young lady.

[*She goes off, right.*]

SIMO: Wouldn't anyone who knows you believe you're at the
bottom of this?

DAVOS: Bottom of what, sir?

SIMO: She didn't give instructions at the bedside about what
was to be done for the mother, but waited to come out and
shout indoors from the street. Really, Davos, do you take
me for such a fool? Do I appear a proper dupe for such bare-
faced trickery? You might at least take the trouble to
pretend I'm a man to be feared if I find out.

DAVOS [*aside*]: He's fooling himself this time, nothing to do
with me.

SIMO: I told you not to be up to your tricks, and I warned you
of the consequences. Have you no sense of shame? What's
the point of it? Did you imagine I'd believe your story that
this woman has just borne Pamphilus a son?

DAVOS [*aside*]: That's where he's wrong, and I see what I can
do.

SIMO: Can't you speak?

DAVOS: What's this about believing? Anyone would think
you hadn't been *told* what would happen.

SIMO: *Did* anyone tell me?

DAVOS: You don't mean to say you found out for yourself it
was all made up?

SIMO: You're laughing at me.

DAVOS: You must have been told; how else could you have
suspected this?

SIMO: I can tell you how: I know *you*.

DAVOS: That's as much as saying I put them up to it.

SIMO: And I'm positive you did.

DAVOS: Really, sir, you've got me all wrong.

SIMO: Have I?

DAVOS: Whenever I try to tell you something, you take me up at once for fooling you.

SIMO: And I suppose I'm wrong?

DAVOS: The result is I daren't open my mouth.

SIMO: One thing I do know: no one has had a baby here.

DAVOS: Quite right, sir! But all the same, it won't be long before someone leaves a baby out here on the doorstep. I'm only telling you this now, sir, so that you can't say you weren't warned, and don't go around afterwards saying that Davos put them up to it and it was one of his tricks. I'd be glad of a change in your opinion of me, I must say.

SIMO: How do you know about this?

DAVOS: I believe what I've heard. A lot of things have given me the idea, and they all hang together. Earlier on, the girl said she was pregnant by Pamphilus, and we've found that's not true. Now she sees preparations for a wedding in your house, so she sends her maid to fetch a midwife and bring in a baby at the same time. She knows if she can't make you see the child that nothing will stop the marriage.

SIMO: Yes, but once you'd discovered this plan, why didn't you tell Pamphilus at once?

DAVOS [virtuously]: Who was it, pray, who got him to break with her if it wasn't me? We all know he used to be crazy about her, but now he's looking for a wife. Just you leave everything to me, sir. Carry on with these wedding arrangements as you are doing, and I only hope the gods are on our side.

SIMO: No, I'd rather you went in. Make all the necessary preparations and wait for me there. [DAVOS goes into SIMO's *house.*] I'm not entirely convinced; and yet perhaps all he said may be true. It doesn't really matter. Much the most important thing is the promise I had from my son's own lips. Now I'll find Chremes and beg him to give us his daughter. If he agrees, what better time for the wedding than today? And if Pamphilus proves unwilling, I'm sure I've every right to put pressure on him to make him keep his promise. Why, here *is* Chremes, just when I want him. [CHREMES *comes on left.*] Chremes, I hope –

CHREMES: Ah, Simo, I was looking for you.

SIMO: As I was for you.

CHREMES [*stiffly*]: I'm glad I've met you. Several people have approached me to say they had heard from you that my daughter is to be married to your son today. I have come to see whether this is a delusion of theirs – or yours.

SIMO [*anxiously*]: Listen a moment, and you'll know why I want you and have the answer to your question.

CHREMES: I'm listening. Say what you like.

SIMO: In the name of heaven, Chremes, and of our friendship which started in boyhood and has increased with our years – in the name of your only daughter and my son whose only chance of salvation rests in your hands – I beg you to help me in this matter and let the marriage take place as it was planned.

CHREMES: Don't beg me – it doesn't take entreaties to win my consent. Do you suppose *I* have changed since the time when I made the offer? If this marriage is going to benefit them both, have her fetched. But if more harm than good will come out of it for either of them, I must ask you to take thought for our joint interests, as if my girl were your own daughter and I were the father of your son.

SIMO: That is precisely the spirit in which I want this marriage, and am pressing for it to take place. I wouldn't do so, Chremes, if I weren't prompted by the facts.

CHREMES: What do you mean?

SIMO: My son has quarrelled with Glycerium.

CHREMES [*sceptically*]: Quite so, quite so.

SIMO: Seriously enough for me to have hopes he will break with her.

CHREMES: Nonsense!

SIMO: It's a fact.

CHREMES: And I can tell you what sort of a fact; lovers' quarrels are a renewal of love.

SIMO: That is exactly what I want to convince you we should forestall. Now is the time, when his passion is stifled while they bandy insults. Before these women's false tears and wicked ways can lure his lovesick mind back to tender feelings, we must marry him off. Once he has a settled relationship with a wife he can respect I am hopeful that he will find it easy to shake off his bad habits.

CHREMES: That's what you think. Personally I don't believe he can. Nor will he be able to carry on with that woman for ever, any more than I can put up with his conduct.

SIMO: How do you know he can't change if you don't make the experiment?

CHREMES: That sort of experiment's too risky for my daughter.

SIMO: But in fact, all the possible disadvantages come to this: there might be a separation, which God forbid. On the other hand, look at all the advantages if he reforms. To begin with, you'll have restored a son to your friend, and then you'll have a steady husband for your daughter and son-in-law for yourself.

CHREMES [*dubiously*]: All right, have it your own way, if

you've convinced yourself that this is a good thing. I don't want to stand in your path.

SIMO: Thank you, Chremes. No wonder I've always had the highest opinion of you.

CHREMES: But I say –

SIMO: What?

CHREMES: How do you know those two really have quarrelled?

SIMO: I had it from Davos himself who knows all their secrets. He's urging me to hurry on the wedding as fast as I can, and you can't think he would do that if he didn't know my son wanted it too. He shall talk to you himself. [*Calling indoors*] Send Davos out here! Here he comes.

[DAVOS *comes out of the house.*]

DAVOS: I was just coming for you, sir.

SIMO: What for?

DAVOS: Why aren't we fetching the bride? It's getting late.

SIMO [*to* CHREMES]: Did you hear that? Now, Davos, I used to have my doubts about you, thinking you might follow the common run of servants and play some trick on me because my son is having an affair.

DAVOS: Should I do such a thing?

SIMO: I was afraid you would, and so I kept from you the truth you are now to hear.

DAVOS: What is it?

SIMO: I'll tell you. [*After a doubtful pause*] I *think* you're to be trusted.

DAVOS: Then you've discovered my true character at last, sir.

SIMO: There wouldn't have been any wedding.

DAVOS: What, no wedding?

SIMO: No. It was all a pretence to test the pair of you.

DAVOS: You don't say so, sir.

SIMO: It's true.

DAVOS: Well I never! I could never have discovered that. What a clever notion!

SIMO: Now listen. After I sent you indoors I had the good fortune to meet my friend Chremes here.

DAVOS [*aside*]: Now we're for it.

SIMO: I told him what you told me just now.

DAVOS [*aside*]: Oh no, no ...

SIMO: I begged him for his daughter, and in the end I won his consent.

DAVOS [*aside*]: I'm done for.

SIMO: What's that you said?

DAVOS [*hastily*]: Delighted, sir, I said I'm delighted.

SIMO: There'll be no further difficulties on his side.

CHREMES: I'll just go home and tell them to get ready and be back to tell you. [*He goes off, left.*]

SIMO: Now, Davos, as your unaided efforts have brought about this marriage, I beg you –

DAVOS [*aside*]: My own unaided efforts!

SIMO: – to set about reforming my son from now on.

DAVOS [*miserably*]: I'll do my best, sir.

SIMO: You'll succeed now, in his present state of irritation with that girl.

DAVOS: Don't you worry any more, sir.

SIMO: Very well then, where is he now?

DAVOS: I suppose he's at home.

SIMO: I'll go and tell him what I've said to you.

[*He goes into his house.*]

DAVOS: And that's the end of *me*. Nothing now to stop me going straight from here to the mill – no chance of begging for mercy. I've messed up everything, deceived my master, pushed his son into marriage, fixed up the wedding for

today – which the old man never expected nor Pamphilus
wanted. Clever, aren't I. If I'd kept quiet there'd have been
none of this trouble. Now here he is. I'm done for. I wish
I'd something to fall on [*with gesture of stabbing himself as*
PAMPHILUS *bursts out of* SIMO's *house*].

PAMPHILUS [*aside*]: Where's that rascal who's destroyed me?

DAVOS: *And* himself.

PAMPHILUS: It's my own fault, I admit, for being such a
stupid fool as to trust my affairs to a useless slave! I'm paying the price for my folly, but he shan't escape unpunished!

DAVOS: I'll keep a whole skin for the rest of my life if I can
only get out of this scrape.

PAMPHILUS: What am I to say to my father now? Refuse to
marry when I've just said I would? I don't think I've the
nerve. . . . I just can't think what to do with myself.

DAVOS: Neither can I, and I'm trying hard. I'd better say I'll
find some way of putting off the evil hour.

PAMPHILUS [*seeing* DAVOS]: Hi, you!

DAVOS: He's seen me.

PAMPHILUS: Look here, my good man, do you realize the
wretched trap your good advice has sprung on me?

DAVOS: I'll soon get you out of it, sir.

PAMPHILUS: Will you, indeed!

DAVOS: Of course I will, sir.

PAMPHILUS: Using the same methods as before, I suppose.

DAVOS: Oh no, sir, I hope to do better this time.

PAMPHILUS: And I'm to trust a rascal like you? How can you
clear up this appalling muddle? Didn't I rely on you? And
now you've taken me out of my peaceful state and pushed
me into marriage. Didn't I tell you this would happen?

DAVOS: You did, sir.

PAMPHILUS: What do you deserve?

DAVOS: Crucifixion. But just give me a moment to recover myself and I'll see daylight.

PAMPHILUS: Damn you, I can't wait now to deal with you as I'd like – I've only got time to look after myself. Your punishment must wait.

[CHARINUS *rushes on left, without seeing them.*]

CHARINUS: Is this credible? A thing to boast of? That men can be so villainous that they delight in evil and seek to profit by the misfortunes of their friends? Can this be true? Yes indeed, it's the lowest class of men who lack the moral courage to say no at the time, but later, when the moment comes for them to carry out their promise, are forced by necessity to reveal their true selves. They may be ashamed, but circumstances drive them to it. And did you ever hear such insolence? 'Who are you?' and 'What do I care?' they say. 'Why should you have my girl? Number one comes first with me.' Suppose you remind them of their promise – you'll soon find they've no scruples when they're needed, but all too many when they're not.

Now what am I to do? Find him and protest about the wrong he's done me? Heap abuse on him? Someone will tell me that gets me nowhere. But it will, quite a bit; at least I shall have annoyed him and relieved my feelings.

PAMPHILUS [*coming forward nervously*]: Charinus, unless heaven helps us I've destroyed us both – but I never meant to.

CHARINUS: 'Never meant to'? Well, there's an excuse at last; you've been as good as your word.

PAMPHILUS: What do you mean, 'at last'?

CHARINUS: Do you imagine you can still lead me on with talk like that?

PAMPHILUS: I don't know what you're talking about.

CHARINUS: It was only *after* I told you I loved her that you

took a fancy to her – the more fool me, to judge your nature
by my own!

PAMPHILUS: You're wrong.

CHARINUS: I suppose you thought there was no solid satisfaction to be won except by deceiving a man in love and
leading him on with false hopes. Very well, take her.

PAMPHILUS: Take her? Oh, you've no idea of all the trouble
I'm in, and the misery and worry that worthless man of
mine has brought about with his schemes!

CHARINUS: Nothing very surprising there – if he takes his
cue from you.

PAMPHILUS: You wouldn't talk like that if you knew me and
my feelings.

CHARINUS: I see; you've just quarrelled with your father, so
now he's angry with you, and he hasn't been able to fix up
your wedding today.

PAMPHILUS: No, no, it's worse than that – and to show you
how little you know of my troubles: this marriage was *not*
being arranged, and no one was trying to provide me with a
wife just now.

CHARINUS [*scornfully*]: I see; you were forced into it – of
your own free will.

PAMPHILUS: Wait – you still don't see –

CHARINUS: I can see quite well that you're going to marry
my girl.

PAMPHILUS: Oh, do stop, you'll drive me mad. Just *listen*. He
never stopped badgering me to tell my father I'd agree to
marry. He begged and prayed till he drove me to it.

CHARINUS: Who are you talking about?

PAMPHILUS: Davos.

CHARINUS: *Davos?*

PAMPHILUS: He's the trouble-maker.

CHARINUS: Why?

PAMPHILUS: I've no idea. All I know is that it was an evil hour for me when I listened to him.

CHARINUS: Is this correct, Davos?

DAVOS [*unwillingly*]: Yes.

CHARINUS: You scoundrel, do you realize what you're saying? God damn you as you deserve! If all his enemies wanted to push him into matrimony, isn't this just what they'd tell him to do? Answer me that.

DAVOS [*with dignity*]: I've been disappointed, but I'm not discouraged.

PAMPHILUS: So I see!

DAVOS: This way hasn't succeeded, so we'll try something else – unless you think that because the first attempt didn't do very well it's impossible to put things right.

PAMPHILUS: Exactly what I do think. And moreover, I'm pretty sure that if you carry on with your efforts, instead of one marriage you'll present me with two.

DAVOS: As your servant, sir, it's my duty to work night and day, hand and foot, and risk my life if only I can be of service to you. If things don't always go according to plan, you only have to forgive me. My efforts may not be successful, sir, but I do my best. Of course if you like, you can think up something better yourself and get rid of me.

PAMPHILUS: That's what I want; but first you'll have to put me back where you found me.

DAVOS: Very good, sir.

PAMPHILUS: And do it *now*.

DAVOS [*playing for time*]: Well ... Just a minute, that's Glycerium's door.

PAMPHILUS: Mind your own business.

DAVOS: I'm thinking. . . .

PAMPHILUS: Really? At last?

DAVOS: And soon I'll have a plan ready for you.

[GLYCERIUM's *door opens and* MYSIS *comes out, talking to her mistress inside.*]

MYSIS: I'll be sure to find your Pamphilus wherever he is and bring him back with me. Now don't you worry yourself, my dear.

PAMPHILUS: Mysis!

MYSIS [*turning round*]: Who's that? Ah, Pamphilus, that's good.

PAMPHILUS: What's the matter?

MYSIS: She told me to beg you, if you love her, my mistress that is, to come to her at once. She's longing to see you, she says.

PAMPHILUS: Oh, this is terrible – it's starting all over again. [*To* DAVOS] All this distress and worry for us both is entirely your doing. She's sending for me now because she's heard of those wedding preparations.

CHARINUS: And how easily you could have kept clear of them if he'd only kept quiet!

DAVOS [*to* CHARINUS]: That's right, send him crazy, if he isn't bad enough already without your interference.

MYSIS [*to* PAMPHILUS]: Yes indeed, sir, that's the very reason why my poor lady's so distressed.

PAMPHILUS [*earnestly*]: Mysis, by all the gods in heaven, I swear to you that I will never desert her, not if I knew that I should make the whole world my enemy. I sought her out and won her; we were made for each other. To hell with those who want to part us! Nothing shall take her from me but death.

MYSIS: I can breathe again.

PAMPHILUS: I assure you, it's as true as the oracle of Apollo! Now, if it's possible to make my father believe that it's

nothing to do with me that the wedding's broken off, all the
better; but if that proves impossible, I'll see that he thinks I
did it, and that's easy. [*Turning to* CHARINUS *for approval*]
What do you think of me?

CHARINUS [*gloomily*]: That you're in trouble, same as me.

DAVOS: I'm thinking up a plan –

PAMPHILUS [*sarcastically*]: Clever boy! I know your efforts –

DAVOS: This one, I tell you, will be all worked out.

PAMPHILUS: Yes, but it's needed *now*.

DAVOS: It's ready.

CHARINUS: What is it?

DAVOS: Let's get this clear: it's for him, not you.

CHARINUS: Oh, all right.

PAMPHILUS [*still sceptical*]: Well then, what will you do?

DAVOS [*with growing importance*]: I doubt if this day's long
    enough for all I have to see to, so don't imagine I've time to
    waste on talking. Take yourselves off, you two, you're in
    my way.

PAMPHILUS: I shall go and see Glycerium.

   [*He goes into her house.*]

DAVOS: And where will *you* go?

CHARINUS: Shall I speak frankly?

DAVOS: Yes, of course. [*Aside*] Here begins a long rigmarole.

CHARINUS: What'll be done for *me*?

DAVOS: You've got a nerve! Isn't it enough that I'm giving
    you a short reprieve, so long as I can postpone this wedding?

CHARINUS: But all the same, Davos –

DAVOS: Well, what?

CHARINUS: Fix up *my* wedding . . .

DAVOS: Don't be silly.

CHARINUS [*moving off, left*]: You'll find me here if you can
    manage anything.

DAVOS: Why should I? I've no plan for you.

CHARINUS: But all the same, if there *is* anything –

DAVOS: All right, I'll come.

CHARINUS: – if there is anything I'll be at home.
  [*He goes off.*]

DAVOS: Now, Mysis, you wait for me here a minute till I come out.

MYSIS: What for?

DAVOS: Because you must.

MYSIS: Be quick.

DAVOS: I'll be back in a minute, I say.
  [*He goes into* GLYCERIUM'*s house.*]

MYSIS: God help us, nothing lasts in this world! I used to think Pamphilus was the greatest blessing my mistress could have, friend, lover and husband, always ready to help with anything, and now look at the sorrow he's brought her, poor dear, more trouble as things are than any good he was to her before. Here's Davos back again. [*The door opens and* DAVOS *comes out, carrying the baby.*] Good heavens, man, what are you doing? Where are you taking the child?

DAVOS: Mysis, I need all your wits and presence of mind now, to help me with this.

MYSIS: What are you going to do?

DAVOS: Take this baby from me quickly and put it on our doorstep.

MYSIS: Mercy me, on the ground?

DAVOS: Take some branches from the altar★ there and spread them under it.

MYSIS: Why don't you do it yourself?

★ There was an altar to 'Apollo of the Streets' outside the street-door of a Greek house.

DAVOS: If I have to swear to my master I didn't put it there, then I can do so with a clear conscience.

MYSIS: I see. I've never known you so particular. Give it to me. [*Takes the baby and dandles it.*]

DAVOS: Hurry up; I want to explain what I'm doing. Heavens above! [*looking left along the street*].

MYSIS [*as she puts the baby on* SIMO's *doorstep*]: What is it?

DAVOS: Here's the bride's father. I'll have to give up my first plan.

MYSIS: I don't know what you're talking about.

DAVOS: I'll have to pretend I've just arrived too from the other direction. [*He hurries off, right.*] Mind what you say backs me up when I need it.

MYSIS: I've no idea what you're up to, or how I can help you all, but as you seem to think I can, I'll stay here. I don't want to spoil your chances.

[CHREMES *comes on, left.*]

CHREMES: I've made all the necessary preparations for my daughter's wedding and now I've come to tell them to fetch her. Why, what's this? Good God, a baby! You there, did you put it here?

MYSIS [*aside*]: Oh, where's Davos?

CHREMES: Answer me!

MYSIS: He's nowhere to be seen. Oh dear, dear me, he's gone and left me.

[DAVOS *re-enters.*]

DAVOS: Gracious me, what a hubbub in the market! Law courts crowded! Food prices up! [*Aside*] What else can I say?

MYSIS [*going to meet him*]: Why on earth did you leave me here alone?

DAVOS [*pretending he has just seen the baby*]: What's this non-

sense? Look here, Mysis, where did this child come from?
Who brought it here?

MYSIS: Are you quite crazy, asking me a question like that?

DAVOS: Who else can I ask? There's no one else.

CHREMES [*aside*]: I wonder where it came from.

DAVOS: Will you answer my question?

MYSIS [*indignantly*]: Oh!

DAVOS [*speaking low*]: Come over here [*taking her aside*].

MYSIS: You're mad. Didn't you –

DAVOS [*low*]: Just you answer my questions – not another
word, or else – [*Aloud*] Abusive, are you? Where did it
come from? [*Low*] Speak up.

MYSIS: Our house.

DAVOS [*laughing*]: Oho! Of course! You can't expect decent
behaviour from a woman like that!

CHREMES [*aside*]: I believe she's a servant of the Andrian
girl's.

DAVOS: Do you think we're the sort of people you can fool
with your tricks?

CHREMES: A good thing I'm here.

DAVOS: Hurry up now and take that baby off our doorstep.
[*Low*] Stop – don't move an inch from where you are.

MYSIS [*bewildered*]: Heaven damn you for terrifying a poor
woman out of her wits!

DAVOS: Do you realize I'm speaking to you?

MYSIS: What do you want?

DAVOS: Must you go on asking? Come on, whose is that
baby you put here? Tell me.

MYSIS: Don't you know?

DAVOS [*low*]: Never mind if I know: answer my question.

MYSIS: It's your master's.

DAVOS: Which one of them?

MYSIS: Pamphilus.

DAVOS: *What*! Pamphilus!

MYSIS: Well, isn't it?

CHREMES: I never liked this marriage, and how right I was.

DAVOS: What a monstrous crime!

MYSIS: What's the fuss about?

DAVOS: Isn't that the baby I saw carried into your house yesterday evening?

MYSIS: You impudent rascal!

DAVOS: It's a fact; I saw Canthara with something under her cloak.

MYSIS: Thank Heaven there were some honest women present to witness the birth!

DAVOS: She doesn't know her man, if she thinks she can get at him with this. 'If Chremes sees a baby on the doorstep he won't allow Pamphilus to marry his daughter' is what she thinks, but believe me, he will, all the more.

CHREMES: Believe me, he won't!

DAVOS: And now I'll have you know that if you don't pick that baby up at once I'll kick it into the middle of the street and roll you in the mud with it.

MYSIS: Mercy me, the man's drunk!

DAVOS: One trick leads straight on to another; now I hear it rumoured that the woman's a citizen of Attica.

CHREMES: What!

DAVOS: And he'll be compelled by law to marry her.

MYSIS: Who ever said she wasn't?

CHREMES: A ludicrous situation, and I was nearly dragged into it unawares.

DAVOS: Who's that speaking? Why, you've come at the right moment, sir. Just listen.

CHREMES: I've heard everything already.

DAVOS: Everything, did you say?

CHREMES: Yes, I was listening from the start.

DAVOS: Oh, were you listening, sir? It's a shocking story! She ought to be done away with. [*To* MYSIS] This is the gentleman I mentioned – Davos isn't the only one you thought you could fool.

MYSIS: Oh dear me, sir, I swear I spoke nothing but the truth.

CHREMES: I know the whole story. Is Simo at home?

DAVOS: Yes, sir.

[CHREMES *goes into* SIMO'S *house*.]

MYSIS: Don't touch me, you brute. I'm going straight to my lady –

DAVOS [*stopping her*]: You stupid woman, don't you know what we've done?

MYSIS: How can I know?

DAVOS: That's the father-in-law. It was the only way of telling him what we want him to know.

MYSIS: What? You might have told me before.

DAVOS: Can't you see the difference between spontaneous behaviour which is natural and a put-up job?

[CRITO *comes on left, a middle-aged countryman dressed for travelling.*]

CRITO [*looking round*]: This is the street they say Chrysis lived in, when she preferred riches here acquired by dishonest means to honourable poverty in her own country. Now she's dead, and all her wealth is mine by law. Ah, here's someone I can ask. Good evening.

MYSIS: Mercy me, who's that? Isn't it Chrysis' cousin Crito? Yes, it is.

CRITO: Mysis! How are you?

MYSIS: And how are you, sir?

CRITO: Is it true that Chrysis –

MYSIS: Alas, we've lost her.

CRITO: And the rest of you? How are you managing here? Fairly well?

MYSIS: Oh, as well as we can, as they say, since it can't be as well as we'd like.

CRITO: What about Glycerium? Has she found her parents yet?

MYSIS [*sighing*]: If only she had!

CRITO: Not yet? I seem to have chosen a bad moment. If I'd known, of course I would never have come. She was always thought and spoken of as Chrysis' sister, and now she's in possession of her property. I'm a stranger here, and I know quite well from other people's experience just how *easy* and *useful* it will be for me to go to law. At the same time I expect she's found a friend and protector already, for she must be quite a big girl by now. I'll only get myself talked about for sharp practice and meanness and legacy-hunting . . . and in any case I shouldn't want to leave her penniless.

MYSIS: There's an honest man for you! The same old Crito.

CRITO: Take me to see her, now I'm here.

MYSIS: With pleasure, sir.

[*They go into* GLYCERIUM's *house.*]

DAVOS: I'll come too. I don't want my old man to see me just yet.

[*He follows them in. There is a short pause, and then* CHREMES *and* SIMO *come out of* SIMO's *house.*]

CHREMES: You've had ample proof of my friendly feeling for you, Simo, and I've been running quite enough risks. Please stop trying to persuade me. In my willingness to fall in with your wishes I nearly gambled away my daughter's life.

SIMO: No, no, Chremes. I must beg and pray you now more than ever to carry out the promise you made me just now.

CHREMES: See how unreasonable your obstinacy makes you. As long as you can get what you want you don't think what you're asking of me, or whether there should be limits to good-nature. If you paused to think, you would stop trying to wear me down with your unjust demands.

SIMO: What demands?

CHREMES: Need you ask? You forced me to promise my daughter to a young man who is completely wrapped up in a love-affair and has no interest in taking a wife. She faces the prospect of quarrels in the home and the break-up of her marriage, simply so that your son can be cured by *her* pain and distress. You got your way, and I agreed to the arrangement while the situation made it possible: Now that has changed, and you must put up with it. People are saying that his mistress is a free citizen; and now there's a baby born. That settles it, as far as we're concerned.

SIMO: For Heaven's sake don't allow yourself to believe them! Their only interest is to present the boy in the worst possible light. All these schemes and false rumours are only intended to put an end to his marriage. Remove their motive and they'll soon stop.

CHREMES: You're wrong. I was present myself when the woman's servant was quarrelling with Davos.

SIMO [*impatiently*]: Yes, yes, I know.

CHREMES: Quite openly too, as neither of them was aware of my presence.

SIMO: I know, I know, Davos told me what the women would do. I meant to tell you, but somehow I forgot.

[DAVOS *comes out of* GLYCERIUM's *house, talking back to her.*]

DAVOS: I tell you there's no need to worry now –

CHREMES: There you are, there's Davos.

SIMO [*indignantly*]: Coming out of that house!

DAVOS: – thanks to me, with the help of the foreign gentleman.

SIMO: Now what's he up to?

DAVOS: I've never seen anything so opportune! Man, arrival, time –

SIMO: The rascal! Who can he mean?

DAVOS: Everything safe with a happy landing.

SIMO [*moving towards him*]: I'll speak to him.

DAVOS [*aside*]: It's the master! What shall I do?

SIMO: Well, Davos, my good man –

DAVOS [*hastily*]: Oh sir, and you too, sir, everything's ready indoors.

SIMO: You've done well.

DAVOS: You can fetch the lady whenever you like.

SIMO: Very good. That's all we need. [*Grimly*] And now: will you kindly tell me what took you into that house?

DAVOS [*taken aback*]: M-me, sir?

SIMO: Yes, you.

DAVOS: M-me?

SIMO: So I said.

DAVOS: I just went in –

SIMO: I'm not asking you *when* you went in.

DAVOS: – with your son.

SIMO: What! Is Pamphilus in there now? Oh, this is too much to bear! Didn't you tell me they had quarrelled, you wretch?

DAVOS: So they have.

SIMO: Then what's he doing there?

CHREMES [*sarcastically*]: What do you suppose? Quarrelling, no doubt.

DAVOS [*trying to recover himself*]: No, sir, please, I'll have to tell you some shocking news. An old man came here just now – and he's in there now – impudent and artful – to look at him you'd think him worth the earth, with his face all stiff and solemn and an honest way of talking –

SIMO: What's he got to do with us?

DAVOS: Nothing, sir, except for what I heard him say.

SIMO: And what was that?

DAVOS: He said he knew Glycerium was a citizen of Attica.

SIMO: Did he! [*Crossing to his house and opening the door*] Dromo! Dromo!

DAVOS: What's the matter, sir?

SIMO: Dromo!

DAVOS: Listen, sir –

SIMO: If you say another word – Dromo!

DAVOS: Sir, do please listen –

    [*The servant* DROMO *comes out.*]

DROMO: What is it, sir?

SIMO: Take him in and string him up, quick as you can.

DROMO: Who?

SIMO: Davos.

DROMO: Why?

SIMO: Because I say so. Go on, take him.

DAVOS: What have I done?

SIMO: Take him away.

DAVOS: If you find anything I've said isn't true, you can kill me, sir.

SIMO: I'm not listening.

DROMO [*menacingly*]: I'll tickle you up a bit, see?

DAVOS [*struggling in* DROMO'S *grasp*]: Even if I'm proved right?

SIMO: Yes. [*To* DROMO] See that he's kept tied up, and listen! Tie him hands-to-feet. Go on! And as sure as I live I'll show you and Pamphilus here and now what a dangerous game

you've been playing, thinking you could deceive me –
your master and his father.

[DROMO *hustles* DAVOS *in.*]

CHREMES: Please don't be so violent.

SIMO: Oh, Chremes, my undutiful child! You should be
sorry for me. So much trouble I've taken for such a son!
[*Opening* GLYCERIUM'*s door and shouting*] Here, Pamphilus!
Come out, Pamphilus! Have you no shame?

[PAMPHILUS *hurries out.*]

PAMPHILUS: Who wants me? How awful, it's my father.

SIMO: What's that, you –

CHREMES: Never mind about abusing him, stick to facts.

SIMO: Could any words be too harsh for him? Do you dare to
tell me that girl is a free-born citizen?

PAMPHILUS: So they say.

SIMO: 'So they say'? What impudence! Does he think what
he's saying? Is he ashamed of his conduct? Look at him –
does any sign of a blush mark his shame? Is he so lacking in
self-control that he ignores his country's laws and customs
and defies his father's wishes simply because he has set his
heart on possessing this woman – to his everlasting disgrace?

PAMPHILUS [*overwhelmed*]: I'm a miserable wretch!

SIMO [*warming up to his scene*]: What? Have you only just
realized that, Pamphilus? At the time when you made up
your mind to satisfy your desires, no matter how – *that* was
the moment for these words to fit you. What about *me*?
Why should I suffer? Why dwell in torment? Why harass
my old age with the folly of a boy like this? Must I pay the
penalty for his misdeeds? No, no, let him keep her and live
with her; I'll bid him good-bye.

PAMPHILUS: Father!

SIMO: Why call me Father? Have you any need of me as a

father? Home, wife and children you have found for yourself, against your father's wishes. You've brought your witnesses to swear she is free-born; you win, I lose.

PAMPHILUS: Father, may I just say something –

SIMO: What can you say – to me?

CHREMES: Hear him, Simo, all the same.

SIMO: Hear him, Chremes? What am I to hear?

CHREMES: Just let him speak.

SIMO: Very well, he can speak.

PAMPHILUS [with emotion]: I admit I love her, and if that is doing wrong, then I admit that too. I surrender, father. Give me your orders, lay on me what burdens you like. Do you want me to marry? And must I send her away? I'll bear this somehow, as well as I can. Only one thing I beg of you; don't believe that I had anything to do with this old gentleman's coming here. Let me bring him out to meet you and clear myself.

SIMO: Bring him out here?

PAMPHILUS: Please, Father.

CHREMES: It's a reasonable request. You ought to grant it.

PAMPHILUS: Please don't refuse.

SIMO: All right. [PAMPHILUS goes into GLYCERIUM's house.] Anything to find out that he's not deceiving me, Chremes.

CHREMES: A father shouldn't be too hard on his children whatever their faults.

[CRITO and PAMPHILUS come out, talking.]

CRITO: Say no more. Any one of these is a good enough reason for my doing what you want – consideration for you, goodwill towards Glycerium, or the simple truth.

CHREMES: Why, isn't that Crito from Andros? Yes, it is.

CRITO: Chremes! I hope I find you well.

CHREMES: You're a rare visitor to Athens. What brings you here?

CRITO: Oh, just chance. Is this Simo?

CHREMES: It is.

CRITO [*advancing with outstretched hand*]: Simo –

SIMO [*ignoring this*]: Do you want me? Here, is it you who say that Glycerium's a free-born citizen?

CRITO: Are you saying she's not?

SIMO: You've come here properly primed, haven't you?

CRITO: What do you mean?

SIMO: You know very well. Do you expect to get away with this? Coming here and leading young men astray who've been properly brought up and are ignorant of the world, working on their minds with temptations and promises?

CRITO: Are you in your right mind?

SIMO: Tying up affairs with kept women in the bonds of matrimony?

PAMPHILUS [*aside*]: Oh dear, I'm afraid he'll never stand up to this.

CHREMES: If you knew my friend properly, Simo, you would not think this of him. He's an honest man.

SIMO: *He*'s an honest man? When he turned up so smartly the very day of the wedding, though he's never been here before? Yes, yes, Chremes, just the sort of man to trust.

PAMPHILUS [*aside*]: If I weren't so afraid of my father there's a bit of good advice I could give him.

SIMO: Impostor!

CRITO: What!

CHREMES: It's just his manner, Crito. Take no notice.

CRITO: Let him mind his manners. If he persists in talking to me exactly as he likes, he will hear a few things that he *won't* like. [*To* SIMO] I'm not interfering with your affairs;

they're no concern of mine. They're *your* troubles; grin and
bear them! Anyway, we can soon find out whether the
information I gave you was true or false. Some time ago a
citizen of Attica was shipwrecked on the coast of Andros.
With him was a small girl – the woman we're talking about.
He lost everything, and the first person he approached for
help happened to be Chrysis' father.

SIMO [*scornfully*]: Here the story starts.

CHREMES: Let him go on.

CRITO: Why is he interrupting?

CHREMES: Continue.

CRITO: Moreover, this man who gave him shelter was a relative of mine, and it was in his house that the stranger told
me himself that he was an Attic citizen; there too he died.

CHREMES [*eagerly*]: His name?

CRITO: Dear, dear, sprung on me like that . . . was it Phania?
Yes, Phania, I'm almost certain it was. I'm quite positive
anyway that he said he came from Rhamnus.

CHREMES [*aside*]: Heavens above!

CRITO: All this was known to a lot of other people in Andros
at the time.

CHREMES [*aside*]: Maybe . . . Dare I hope? [*To* CRITO] Quick,
tell me, what did he say about the girl? Was she his daughter?

CRITO: He said not.

CHREMES: Whose was she then?

CRITO: His brother's.

CHREMES: It's true! She's mine!

CRITO: What!

SIMO: What's that, Chremes?

PAMPHILUS [*aside*]: Mark this, Pamphilus.

SIMO: What makes you think so?

CHREMES: Phania was my brother.

SIMO: Of course he was. I knew him.

CHREMES: He left Athens to get away from the war and intended to follow me across to Asia. He was afraid to leave the girl here at such a time. Since then I've never heard what happened to him until today.

PAMPHILUS: Oh, I'm beside myself for joy, my head's in a whirl with hope and fear and delight at this marvellous, unexpected, immense good fortune!

SIMO [to CHREMES]: I'm delighted too in every way that she's found to be your daughter.

PAMPHILUS: I'm sure you are, Father.

CHREMES: There's still just one small thing which worries me.

PAMPHILUS [aside]: Oh, you and your scruples, you tiresome old fool; you'd look for knots in a bulrush.

CRITO: What is it?

CHREMES: The name's not right.

CRITO: She had a different one when she was small.

CHREMES: What was it, Crito? Can't you remember?

CRITO: I'm trying to think. . . .

PAMPHILUS [impatiently]: I'm not going to have my happiness held up by his memory when the remedy's in my own hands. Listen, Chremes, the name you want is Pasibula.

CHREMES: Right!

CRITO: That's it.

PAMPHILUS: She's told me it thousands of times herself.

SIMO: I am sure you know that we are all delighted about this, Chremes.

CHREMES: Indeed I do.

PAMPHILUS: And now, Father –

SIMO: The truth has reconciled me to everything.

PAMPHILUS [hugging him]: Father, you're splendid. And as

regards my right to possess her? Chremes doesn't raise any objection as I've already had her.

CHREMES [*drily*]: On the contrary, that's an excellent reason; so long as your father agrees.

PAMPHILUS: Of course there's the –

SIMO: Yes indeed.

CHREMES: Her dowry is sixty thousand drachmas, Pamphilus.

PAMPHILUS: I accept.

CHREMES: I can't wait to see my daughter. Come with me, Crito – I suppose she won't know me.

SIMO: Why not have her brought over to my house?

PAMPHILUS: A good suggestion! I'll tell Davos to see to it at once.

> [CHREMES *and* CRITO *go into* GLYCERIUM'*s house.*]

SIMO: That's impossible.

PAMPHILUS: Why?

SIMO: There's something more urgent – for which he's better suited – that's stopping him.

PAMPHILUS: What's that?

SIMO: He's tied up.

PAMPHILUS [*indignantly*]: I don't think that was a proper thing to do, Father.

SIMO: Well, I told them to do it properly.

PAMPHILUS: Tell them to undo him, please.

SIMO: All right.

PAMPHILUS: Quickly!

SIMO: I'm just going.

> [*He goes into his house.*]

PAMPHILUS: Oh what a lovely lucky day!

> [CHARINUS *comes on, left.*]

CHARINUS: I just want to see how Pamphilus is getting on. Why, there he is.

PAMPHILUS [*not seeing him*]: Some people might fancy I
think this too good to be true, but I want to believe it and I
shall! If the gods enjoy eternal life I'm sure it's because their
joys are everlasting, so my immortality is won so long as
trouble doesn't interrupt my happiness. But who do I want
here most to hear the news?

CHARINUS: What's he so happy about?

[DAVOS *comes out, rubbing his arms and shoulders.*]

PAMPHILUS: Here's Davos, he's the man I want. He's the only
one who'll be genuinely glad to see me happy.

DAVOS: Where's Pamphilus?

PAMPHILUS: Davos!

DAVOS: Who's that?

PAMPHILUS: It's me.

DAVOS: Oh sir –

PAMPHILUS: You don't know what's happened to me!

DAVOS: No, I don't. But I know what's happened to *me*.

PAMPHILUS [*patting him on the shoulder*]: So do I.

DAVOS: There you are, you've heard of my troubles before I
know your good news; the usual thing.

PAMPHILUS: My Glycerium has found her parents!

DAVOS [*genuinely pleased*]: That's good.

CHARINUS: What!

PAMPHILUS: Her father's a great friend of ours.

DAVOS: Who is he?

PAMPHILUS: Chremes.

DAVOS: That's splendid news.

PAMPHILUS: There's nothing to stop me marrying her now.

CHARINUS [*aside*]: His heart's desire! Can he be dreaming?

PAMPHILUS: Then there's the baby, Davos –

DAVOS: That's enough, sir. He's sure to be first favourite of
the gods.

CHARINUS [coming forward]: If this is true – it'll save my life.
　　I'll speak to them.
PAMPHILUS: Who's that? Charinus, just when we want you!
CHARINUS: Congratulations.
PAMPHILUS: Did you hear?
CHARINUS: Everything. And now, have a thought for me in
　　your good fortune. You've got Chremes just where you
　　want him – I'm sure he'll do anything for you.
PAMPHILUS: I haven't forgotten you. What's more, it would
　　take too long if we wait for him to come out.* Come in
　　with me – he's there now with Glycerium. Davos, you
　　hurry home and send people to bring her over to us. Come
　　on, be quick, don't stand about.

　　[PAMPHILUS and CHARINUS go into GLYCERIUM's
　　house.]
DAVOS: I'm going. [To the audience] You needn't wait for
　　them to come out again; the other betrothal and any other
　　business will take place in there. Just give us your applause.
　　[He goes into SIMO's house.]

ALTERNATIVE ENDING

(The following lines exist in some late MSS., written at the end of
the play, but originally intended to follow line 976. They were
known to the commentators Donatus and Eugraphius, who agree
that they were not by Terence, but it is impossible to determine when
and by whom they were written.)

　　[CHREMES comes out of the house; CHARINUS and DAVOS
　　stand aside.]
PAMPHILUS: Ah, Chremes, I was waiting for you. I'd like to
　　talk to you about a matter which concerns you, and I'm

　　　　　* Alternative ending starts from here.

anxious for you not to say that I've forgotten your other daughter. I believe I've found a husband for her who will suit both you and her.

CHARINUS: I can't bear this, Davos. My love and life are both at stake.

CHREMES: There's nothing new in your proposal, Pamphilus; I could have agreed long ago if I'd wanted it.

CHARINUS: There, I'm done for, Davos.

DAVOS: Wait a bit.

CHARINUS: I'm finished.

CHREMES: But I'll tell you why I didn't want it. It wasn't because I was altogether against the young man –

CHARINUS: What?

DAVOS: Hush.

CHREMES: – but because I wanted the friendship which Simo and I inherited from our fathers to be passed on to our children not diminished but strengthened. But now that I have the opportunity and good fortune to make both my daughters happy, I give my consent.

PAMPHILUS: That's fine.

DAVOS: Come and thank him.

CHARINUS [*coming forward*]: Good evening, Chremes, kindest of friends! It's as great a pleasure to have learnt what you thought of me as it is to succeed in obtaining what I've wanted so much.

CHREMES: You can be sure my feelings, Charinus, match your own heart-felt desires; and from your knowledge of me you can infer that in spite of my lack of friendliness I knew your worth.

CHARINUS: I see.

CHREMES: And so I promise you my daughter Philumena for your wife, with a dowry of thirty-six thousand drachmas.

THE SELF-TORMENTOR

[HEAUTON TIMORUMENOS]

INTRODUCTORY NOTE

The Self-Tormentor is listed as Terence's third play and was performed in 163 B.C., whereas *The Eunuch*, listed as second, was not performed until 161. It is not clear why *The Eunuch* was held back. The success of *The Girl from Andros* had been followed by the first failure of *The Mother-in-Law*, and Terence may have been unwilling to follow on at once with *The Eunuch*, and then decided to bring out first the play he had been writing during the two-year interval.

It is a puzzling play in more than one sense. Terence warns us in the Prologue that there is little action and everything depends on the dialogue, and it is indeed the least dramatic, but the most logical, of all the plays. It demands hard concentration on the part of an audience if they are not to be as confused as Syrus' dupes by the complexities of double plot and counter-plot, and many may feel that here the clever young playwright has overreached himself. But there is a certain astringency about the dialogue, and the sort of logic one enjoys following in reading the exchanges of Ivy Compton-Burnett's highly articulate characters.

Of the characters, Syrus is a typical nimble-witted young slave who endeavours to carry on several intrigues simultaneously and can generally think of an alternative when one plan fails, and Clinia's feeling for Antiphila is treated romantically in a way which recalls *The Girl from Andros*. The main interest concentrates in the pair of older men, who are as clearly differentiated as Demea and Micio in *The Brothers*. The effect of the intrigues on them interests Terence more than the actual progress of the intrigue (contrast *Phormio*). Chremes in the earlier scenes is always sure he is right and in control of the situation and has to be made to recognize his self-delusion; Menedemus' self-mortification and settled melancholy gradually slip from him until in the end he obviously enjoys turning the tables on Chremes and repeating his own advice to his self-appointed mentor.

It was a popular play in antiquity, much quoted by Cicero, and also by Horace and Seneca. A reference to Menedemus' shabby dress in Varro (*Rerum Rusticarum*, II. ii) suggests that it was still staged in his day. Yet this is the play which is not only the least dramatic but the one which bears traces of careless adaptation. At line 170 Chremes makes a very awkward exit, ostensibly to invite a neighbour, Phania, who plays no part in the play, and the stage is left empty. (A later hand suggested that the interval might be filled by a dance of dinner-guests.) Again, at line 497 Chremes mentions a boundary-dispute between neighbours, and goes off only to return a few lines later. This is quite irrelevant to the play, and one cannot help feeling that it was something Terence took over from a scene where it might have had more point. But it remains a puzzle why such a careful craftsman did not remove these irrelevancies on revision, especially in this elaborately constructed 'literary' play.

The title also suggests that Terence moved away from his original without considering that 'The Self-Tormentor' was not really very apt as a title for the comedy in its final form. After the first scene the interest largely shifts from the inner conflicts of Menedemus to the progressive stages of the discomfiture of Chremes – who may well be Terence's own creation as an addition to the main character of the single-plot original.

PRODUCTION NOTICE

THE SELF-TORMENTOR by Terence: performed at the Megalesian Games* during the curule aedileship of Lucius Cornelius Lentulus and Lucius Valerius Flaccus.

Produced by Lucius Ambivius Turpio and Lucius Atilius of Praeneste.

Music composed by Flaccus, slave of Claudius, at the first performance for unmatched pipes, afterwards for two right-hand pipes.

Greek original by Menander.

The author's third play, written during the consulship of Manius Juventus and Titus Sempronius.†

   *Celebrated annually on 4 April in honour of the Great Mother, the goddess Cybele.

  †i.e. 163 B.C.

SYNOPSIS

Clinia, who is in love with Antiphila, was forced to serve abroad as a soldier by his stern father, who afterwards tortured himself with remorse for his action. Clinia returns, and, unknown to his father, goes to stay with Clitipho, lover of the courtesan, Bacchis. When Clinia sends for Antiphila in his longing to see her, Bacchis appears on the scene as if she were his mistress, with Antiphila dressed as her servant. This was all arranged to enable Clitipho to deceive his father, from whom, by means of Syrus' tricks, he obtains a thousand drachmas for Bacchis. Antiphila is recognized as Clitipho's sister and Clinia marries her, while Clitipho finds another wife.

AUTHOR'S PROLOGUE TO
THE SELF-TORMENTOR
(Spoken by Lucius Ambivius Turpio★)

Some of you may be wondering why the author has given an old man the part usually assigned to a young actor. I will explain this before going on to the speech I am here to deliver. Today I am presenting *The Self-Tormentor*, a fresh comedy from a fresh Greek source, a double plot made out of a single one. Having told you it is a new play and given its name, I should go on to say who wrote it and who wrote the Greek original, if I didn't think most of you know already. Now I'll say briefly why you see me in this part. The author wanted me to represent him, instead of delivering the usual prologue; he has called on you to be his judges and me to plead his case. But I wonder whether my eloquence in delivering this speech can match his skill in marshalling his thoughts when he wrote it for me.

As to the malicious rumours that he creates a few Latin plays by taking a lot of Greek ones and 'spoiling' them for others, he doesn't deny this; in fact he is quite unrepentant and declares he will do the same again. He has good precedent, and sees no reason why he shouldn't follow it in doing what others have done.

Then there's the assertion of that malevolent old playwright† that he took to drama too suddenly, and depends on the talents of his friends rather than on his native genius. This is something which your judgement and opinion will have to decide,

★Terence's actor-producer.
†Luscius Lanuvinus, Terence's rival.

and that is why I want to appeal to you all not to listen to the voice of prejudice instead of that of honest truth. Be fair to authors, and when you are given the opportunity to see something new and free from faults, give them in return a chance to get on in the world. There is one author who needn't think this applies to him – I mean the one who showed us that scene the other day with a running slave pushing his way through a crowd: why further the interests of anyone so crazy? My author will have more to say about his faults when he puts on further new plays, unless the other puts a stop to his slanderous remarks.

Now listen with open minds, don't interrupt, and allow me to present a play which doesn't depend on action. I'm getting on in years, and can't always be shouting at the top of my voice and wearing myself out playing running slaves, angry old men, greedy spongers, shameless impostors and rapacious pimps. Put yourselves in the mood to see the justice of this, if only for my sake, and give me some respite from my labours, for the writers of the new plays today have no consideration for an elderly man like me; they come running to me if they have an exacting part, while the easy ones go to some other company.

This play you are going to see depends purely on its dialogue, so you will be able to see what my talents can do in either style. Let me set a precedent, so that young authors will have to work to please you, their audience, rather than themselves.

CHARACTERS

CHREMES   *an Athenian gentleman*
MENEDEMUS   *his neighbour in the country*
CLITIPHO   *son of Chremes*
CLINIA   *son of Menedemus*
SYRUS   *a slave, attendant on Clitipho*
DROMO   *a slave, attendant on Clinia*
BACCHIS   *a courtesan, mistress of Clitipho*
ANTIPHILA   *a young girl, beloved by Clinia*
SOSTRATA   *wife of Chremes*
PHRYGIA   *maidservant of Bacchis*
A nurse in the household of Chremes

★

The scene is laid in Attica, in front of the farmhouses of Chremes
and Menedemus. To the audience's right the road leads to Athens,
to their left further into the country

[MENEDEMUS, *haggard and shabbily dressed, is wearily breaking clods in the field by his house when his neighbour* CHREMES *comes out of his house to speak to him.*]

CHREMES [*in some embarrassment as* MENEDEMUS *takes no notice*]: I know it's not long since we became acquainted, in fact it all started with your buying the farm next to mine, and this is the first time we've really had much to do with each other. . . . All the same, there's something about you – or maybe it's the fact that we're neighbours, which I always think is the next best thing to being friends – which makes me feel that I ought to speak out. [*He waits until* MENEDEMUS *looks up.*] To be quite frank, your behaviour doesn't seem to me to be right for a man of your age and circumstances. What does it all mean, for heaven's sake? What on earth do you want? You're sixty, if not more, I imagine, and no one hereabouts has better land worth more than yours; you've plenty of slaves to work it, and yet you continue to do their work as if you'd no one at all. However early I go out in the morning, however late I come home in the evening, I always see you out at work, digging or ploughing or moving something about. You never slack off for a moment or think of yourself, and it isn't as if you get any pleasure out of it, I'm sure. You may tell me you're not satisfied with the amount of work done on the place, but if you'd only apply the effort you spend on doing everything yourself to making your people get on with it, you'd do better.

MENEDEMUS: Chremes, can you spare a moment from your

own affairs to listen to someone else's – even if they don't really concern you?

CHREMES: I'm human, so any human interest *is* my concern. Call it solicitude or curiosity on my part, whichever you like. If you're right I'll copy you, and if you're wrong I'll try to make you mend your ways.

MENEDEMUS: This is something I *have* to do; you can do what suits your case.

CHREMES: Does anyone have to torment himself?

MENEDEMUS: Yes, I do.

CHREMES: If you're in trouble, I'm sorry. But what's wrong? What can you have done to deserve this?

MENEDEMUS [*sighs*]

CHREMES: Come now, cheer up; let me know your trouble whatever it is. Don't be afraid to tell me everything, you can trust me. I'll give you all the comfort or advice or practical help I can.

MENEDEMUS [*struggling with his tears*]: Do you really want to know?

CHREMES: Yes, of course I do, for the reason I've just given you.

MENEDEMUS: I'll tell you ...

CHREMES: Then just put down that mattock★ while you do so, and stop working.

MENEDEMUS: No!

CHREMES: Don't be so silly.

MENEDEMUS: You shan't stop me if I refuse to take time off from my labours.

CHREMES [*cheerfully, as he takes the mattock*]: Well, I am stopping you.

★ The heavy pronged hoe still used for breaking up clods by peasant-farmers.

MENEDEMUS [*hopelessly*]: Oh, it's wrong of you.

CHREMES [*leaning the mattock against the wall*]: My goodness, what a weight!

MENEDEMUS: No more than I deserve.

CHREMES: Now then, tell me.

MENEDEMUS: I have an only son, just a boy . . . No, Chremes, I did have one, but whether I still have him or not I've no idea.

CHREMES: What do you mean?

MENEDEMUS: I'll tell you. There's a foreigner here from Corinth, an old woman of humble means. My son fell madly in love with her daughter, in fact he practically treated the girl as his wife. I knew nothing of this at first, but when I did find out I could have shown some humanity and decency in my handling of the boy's love-sick feelings. Instead of which I took the harsh line that parents commonly do in these cases, and was on at him every day. 'Do you hope you'll be allowed to carry on much longer like this in your father's lifetime, setting up a mistress almost as if she were a wife? If that's your idea,' I said, 'you're wrong, Clinia; you don't know me. I'm willing for you to be called my son just as long as you do what's proper in your position – if you don't, I'll find the proper way to deal with you. There's a simple explanation for all this: you haven't got enough to do. When I was your age I'd no thought of love – no, I was a poor man and went off to Asia on active service, and there I won fame and fortune.' The result was that in the end the boy just couldn't stand having the same things dinned into him, and he thought my age and concern for him made me wiser and better able to judge his interests than he could himself. So he went off to Asia to serve in the king's army.

CHREMES: No!

MENEDEMUS: He left without a word to me and has been gone three months.

CHREMES: You're both to blame, though his venture does show spirit as well as respect for you.

MENEDEMUS: When I found this out from the friends who were in his confidence, I came home utterly miserable, almost out of my mind with anxiety and grief. I sat down, and my servants came running to take off my shoes. I saw the others hurrying about, making up a couch, preparing my dinner, everyone doing his best to relieve my distress, and watching them made me think: 'Are all these people worrying solely on my account, just to give me satisfaction? Do I need all these maids to look after my clothes? Must I spend so much on a house for myself, when my only son who should have had half of everything – or even more, as he's at a better age to enjoy it – has been driven from home, poor boy, by my own injustice? Why, I'll deserve any fate if I continue like this. As long as he leads that wretched existence far away from home, and all because of the wrong I did him, I'll do penance for it; I'll toil and save and scrape and slave for him.' That's what I've been doing ever since. I've kept nothing in the house, not a dish nor a rag, collected all I had, all the slaves too, man and woman, except those who could easily earn their keep working in the fields, and auctioned and sold the lot. I put up my house for immediate sale and made about 90,000 drachmas, bought this bit of land, and here I'm working. I've made up my mind that I can lessen the wrong done to my boy by making myself miserable, and I've no right to enjoy any pleasure here until he's safely home to share it with me.

CHREMES: I think you've the makings of a considerate father,

and he could be an obedient son if he were tactfully handled
in the right way. But somehow you've never succeeded in
knowing each other, for the usual reason: lack of sincerity
in your way of life. You never showed him how much he
meant to you, and he didn't dare trust you as a son should
his father. If you had done, this would never have happened.

MENEDEMUS: You're right, I admit. I've made a terrible mistake.

CHREMES: But I'm hopeful for the future, Menedemus. I feel
certain he'll soon come back to you safe and sound.

MENEDEMUS: I pray he will!

CHREMES: Your prayer'll be answered. Come now, it's a
public holiday;* spend the day with me, if it's convenient.

MENEDEMUS: I can't.

CHREMES: Why not? Do please relax, only for a little while;
your son would want it even though he's not here.

MENEDEMUS: I forced him to hard labour. It's not right for
me to shirk it now.

CHREMES: You've made up your mind then?

MENEDEMUS: Yes.

CHREMES: Then I'll say good-bye.

MENEDEMUS: Good-bye.

　　　[*He picks up the mattock and goes off, left.*]

CHREMES: He brings tears to my eyes, I'm so sorry for him.
But it's getting late; high time I reminded my neighbour
Phania about coming to dinner. I'll go and see if he's at
home.

　　　[*He goes off, right. After a short interval when music is played
　　　and dinner-guests assemble and enter* CHREMES' *house,*
　　　CHREMES *returns.*]

CHREMES: He didn't need reminding; they say he's been at

　　　　　　　*The festival of Dionysus.

my house some time, so I'm the one who's keeping my guests waiting. I'll go in at once. [*As he turns to go in, the door opens.*] But who's that at my door? Someone's coming out. I'll step aside.

[*His son* CLITIPHO *comes out without seeing him, talking to someone inside.*]

CLITIPHO: There's nothing to worry about so far, Clinia. They're not late yet, and I'm sure she'll be here soon with the messenger. Do stop torturing yourself with imaginary fears.

CHREMES [*aside*]: Who's my son talking to?

CLITIPHO [*overhearing*]: Why, there's Father, the very man I wanted. I'll speak to him. Father, you've come at the right time.

CHREMES: What do you mean?

CLITIPHO: Do you know this neighbour of ours, Menedemus?

CHREMES: Of course I do.

CLITIPHO: Did you realize he has a son?

CHREMES: I'd heard about one. He's in Asia, I believe.

CLITIPHO: No he isn't, Father; he's in our house.

CHREMES: What!

CLITIPHO: He's just arrived. I met him as he left his ship and carried him off to dinner. He and I have always been good friends since we were boys.

CHREMES: This is good news! I'm delighted. I only wish I'd been more pressing with my invitation to Menedemus to join us, so that I could have been the first to give him this unexpected pleasure in my own house. But there's still time.

[*He moves towards* MENEDEMUS' *house.*]

CLITIPHO: No, don't, Father; you mustn't.

CHREMES: Why not?

CLITIPHO: He hasn't made up his mind yet what to do with

himself. He's only just come, and he's full of fears about his father's anger and his girl's feelings for him. He's crazy about her – she's the cause of all this trouble and the reason why he left home.

CHREMES: I know.

CLITIPHO: He's just sent his boy into town with a message for her, and I've sent our Syrus along too.

CHREMES: What has he to say?

CLITIPHO: Clinia? He can only talk about his misery.

CHREMES: *Misery*? Can you imagine anyone *less* miserable? Are there any of the so-called blessings of mankind he doesn't possess? Parents, a safe home, friends, family, relatives, money, he's got the lot. But I suppose these things take their value from the disposition of their owners, blessings if you know how to use them and curses if you don't.

CLITIPHO: But the old father was always difficult, and what I'm afraid of now is that he'll go too far in his anger against his son.

CHREMES: Menedemus? [*Aside*] No, I mustn't speak; it'll help him if his son's afraid of him.

CLITIPHO: What's that you're saying?

CHREMES: I'll tell you. Whatever the situation, your friend ought to have stayed at home. Maybe his father was a bit too strict for his liking, but he could have put up with it. Is there anyone he could bear with if not his own father? Which would have been right – was the son to adapt himself to the father's ways or the father to the son's? As for his accusing his father of harshness, it's not true. Parents are strict pretty much to the same pattern, provided that they're fairly reasonable men. They don't want their boys to take to drink and women and they keep them on a small allowance, but all this is intended to form their character. But

once the mind is the slave of a base passion, Clitipho, in-
evitably it takes to schemes of the same kind. The sensible
thing is look to others for an example you can profit
by.

CLITIPHO [*anxious to cut him short*]: Yes, of course.

CHREMES: I am going in to see what there is for dinner. It's
late, so don't you go far away.

    [*He goes into his house.*]

CLITIPHO: How unfairly all we young men are judged by
our fathers! They think we ought to be old men at birth,
with no interest in the things which appeal to youth. They
try to control us in the light of their present desires, not
those they had at our age. If I ever have a son, you may be
sure he'll find me an easy father. I shan't seek a means of
finding out his faults unless I can forgive them too – not
like my own father, who's always taking cover behind
someone else to express his views. Damn it all, when he's
taken a glass too many he's got plenty to say for himself!
But now it's nothing but 'look to others for an example you
can profit by'; artful, isn't he! Ah, but he little knows that
his words fall on deaf ears! At the moment I'm far more
concerned about my mistress and her 'give me' and 'fetch
me', to which I've no answer. I doubt if there's anyone
worse off than I am. Why, even Clinia here, who's got his
share of trouble, has a decent, well-brought-up girl with
none of the professional's tricks, while mine is masterful and
insolent, prides herself on being a lady, and costs me the
earth. All I can give her at present is a soft answer, for I can't
bring myself to confess I'm penniless. I've only just realized
it myself, and my father hasn't found out yet.

    [CLINIA *comes out of* CHREMES' *house, looking anxiously
down the road.*]

CLINIA: If I had any luck in loving I'm sure they'd have been here long ago, but I'm terribly afraid someone seduced her while I was away. I keep thinking of things which add to my worry – opportunity, situation, her youth, and the fact that she's under the thumb of her wicked old mother who cares for nothing but cash.

CLITIPHO: Clinia!

CLINIA: I'm so miserable . . .

CLITIPHO: Do please be careful, or someone coming out of your father's house might see you.

CLINIA: All right; but I'm certain there's trouble brewing for me.

CLITIPHO: Do you *have* to be sure of that before you know the facts?

CLINIA: If it weren't trouble they'd be here by now.

CLITIPHO: They'll be here soon.

CLINIA: What do you mean by 'soon'?

CLITIPHO: You forget she's got a long way to come, and you know what women are. Plans and preparations can take them a year.

CLINIA: I'm so nervous, Clitipho.

CLITIPHO [*looking down road, right*]: You can breathe again. Here come Dromo and Syrus; and there are the girls!

[DROMO, *a smart young house-slave, and* SYRUS, *a rather older man, appear from right, and the two couples continue to talk without seeing each other.*]

SYRUS: Really?

DROMO: Yes, truly.

SYRUS [*looking back*]: But while we are talking away like this the girls are left behind.

CLITIPHO: She's here, Clinia. Did you hear that?

CLINIA: Yes, I hear, and now I can see and live again!

DROMO: No wonder, they've got such piles of luggage, and they're bringing a whole troop of servants along.

CLINIA: Damn it, where did she get those from?

CLITIPHO: Don't ask me.

SYRUS: We shouldn't have left them like this. Think what they've got to carry.

CLINIA: Oh, no, no!

SYRUS: All those jewels and dresses; and it's getting dark, and they don't know the way. We've been fools. You go back and meet them, Dromo. Hurry up! What are you waiting for? [DROMO *goes off, right.*]

CLINIA: O misery, the end of all my hopes!

CLITIPHO: What's the matter now? What's worrying you?

CLINIA: Need you ask? Can't you see? Servants, jewels, dresses! And I left her with one little maid. Where do you suppose those came from?

CLITIPHO [*looking down the road*]: Oh, *now* I see.

SYRUS [*also looking*]: My God, what a crowd! I don't believe the house will hold them, and think what they'll eat and drink! Nothing could be worse for my poor old master.
   [*Seeing* CLINIA *and* CLITIPHO]
Ah, there are the two I wanted.

CLINIA [*coming forward*]: God in heaven, where is constancy? I was a homeless wanderer on your account, Antiphila, fool that I was, and you seized your chance meanwhile to get rich and abandon me in my troubles. It's all because of you that I'm in such disgrace and a disobedient son to my father. I'm so ashamed and sorry when I think how he was always warning me about the habits of these women, advice all wasted, for he could never get me to give the girl up. I shall have to do it now, though at the time when I might have been glad to, I refused. No one knows misery like mine.

SYRUS [*aside*]: He seems to have got it all wrong, what we were saying. [*To* CLINIA] Look, sir, you're mistaken about your lady. Her life hasn't changed at all, nor her feelings for you, as far as we could judge from what we saw.

CLINIA: What do you mean, please? There's nothing in the world I'd like better now than to have my suspicions proved false.

SYRUS: First let's make sure you know the whole story. That old woman wasn't her mother, as people used to say, and now she's dead. I happened to hear the girl telling the other one herself as we walked along.

CLITIPHO: What other one?

SYRUS: Wait a bit, sir; let me finish telling the story I began. I'm coming to that later.

CLITIPHO: Be quick, then.

SYRUS: Well, first of all, when we came to the house, Dromo knocked at the door. An old woman came out, and as soon as she'd opened the door, in he darted, with me at his heels. The woman shot the bolt and went back to her spinning. Now, this is where you could have seen as nowhere else, sir, the life she's been leading in your absence; when we burst in on her without warning it gave us a chance to judge her ordinary everyday habits, and that's what best reveals a person's character. We found her busy weaving at her loom, simply dressed and in mourning, I suppose for the old lady who'd died; no sign of jewels, or anything beyond what you'd see on women who dress only to please themselves, with none of those nasty feminine refinements; her hair not done up, but just combed down round her head and carelessly tossed back. I needn't say more.

CLINIA [*clutching him*]: Syrus, dear man, please don't encourage me with false hopes.

SYRUS: The old woman was spinning yarn, and there was only one little maid besides, helping with the weaving, a grubby little slut in rags and tatters.

CLITIPHO: If this is true, Clinia, as I'm sure it is, you're the luckiest man alive! Do you get the point about the maid being shabby and dirty? When go-betweens are uncared-for, it's another positive indication that their mistress is innocent, for it's general practice for men who want access to the mistress to tip the servants first.

CLINIA: Go on, please, Syrus, but don't try to please me on false pretences. What did she say when you mentioned my name?

SYRUS: As soon as we said you were back and asked her to come to you she left her loom at once, tears streaming down her face; it was clear to see how much she had felt your absence.

CLINIA: My God, I don't know where I am for joy! I was terribly afraid.

CLITIPHO: I knew all along there was nothing to be afraid of. Now, Syrus, it's my turn. Who's that other girl?

SYRUS: It's your Bacchis we're bringing along too, sir.

CLITIPHO: *What?* Bacchis? You wretch, where are you taking her?

SYRUS: Where should I? To our house, of course.

CLITIPHO: To meet my father?

SYRUS: Why not?

CLITIPHO [*to* CLINIA]: The brazen impudence of the man!

SYRUS: Look, sir, this is something really serious; you've got to take risks.

CLITIPHO: But are you intending to win glory by gambling on my life? One little slip on your part and I'm finished. [*To* CLINIA] What am I to do with him?

SYRUS: But in fact –

CLITIPHO: What fact?

SYRUS: If you'll let me, I'll tell you.

CLINIA: Let him speak.

CLITIPHO: I'm not stopping him.

SYRUS [*gaining time*]: At present things are – as if – when –

CLITIPHO: Damn the man, must he speak in riddles?

CLINIA: He's right, Syrus. Drop it, and come to the point.

SYRUS [*injured*]: Indeed, I can't keep silence. You're utterly
unfair, sir. I find you quite insufferable.

CLINIA [*forestalling* CLITIPHO]: Do be quiet. We really must
listen to him.

CLITIPHO: Well, what is it?

SYRUS: You want a love-affair, you want your girl and some
ready cash to give her; what you don't want is the risk you
must take to have her. Not bad reasoning, I suppose, if it
really makes sense to cry for the moon. You've got to
accept the bad with the good, or else drop both; these are
the only alternatives, so choose which you like. All the
same, I know my plan's safe and sure, and it'll give you a
chance to have your girl with you in your father's house
with nothing to fear. Then there's the money you've
promised her; I can get it in the same way – you've just
about burst my eardrums going on and on at me to find it.
What more do you want?

CLITIPHO [*dubiously*]: If it really works out . . .

SYRUS: *If* ? Try it and see.

CLITIPHO: Very well, let's hear your plan. What is it?

SYRUS: We'll pretend your girl belongs to Clinia.

CLITIPHO [*with heavy sarcasm*]: Splendid! And what will he
do with his own? Shall she be called his too, in case one isn't
disgrace enough?

SYRUS: We'll hand her over to your mother.

CLITIPHO: Why on earth?

SYRUS: It'd take too long to explain, sir. I've got good reason.

CLITIPHO: Rubbish! I can't see how I gain anything by living in dread like that.

SYRUS: Just a minute, sir. If you're afraid of that plan, I've another, which you'll both admit has no danger at all.

CLITIPHO: That's more like it. Let's hear it, please.

CLINIA: Yes, tell us.

SYRUS: I'll meet them and tell them to return home.

CLITIPHO: *What* did you say?

SYRUS [*injured*]: I'm only trying to remove your fears so that you can sleep sound on either ear.

CLITIPHO: What ever am I to do now?

CLINIA: Well, really –

CLITIPHO: Syrus! Please explain.

SYRUS: Come on, sir; soon you'll be willing when it's too late, and that won't help.

CLINIA: I'd make the best of the situation while you can.

CLITIPHO: Syrus, please –

SYRUS: Do as you like, but I shall stick to what I mean to do. [*Turning to go.*]

CLINIA: It may be your last chance, you know.

CLITIPHO: My God, you're right. Syrus, Syrus! Here, Syrus, come back!

SYRUS [*aside*]: He's warmed up. [*Coming back*] Anything I can do, sir?

CLITIPHO: Come back, come back!

SYRUS: Here I am. Tell me what you want. I suppose you'll soon be saying you don't like that either.

CLITIPHO: No, no, Syrus, I'm putting myself and my love

and reputation in your hands. You're the judge; only take care you don't find yourself in the dock.

SYRUS: That's a silly bit of advice, sir, as if my interests were less at stake than yours. If anything happens to go wrong for us you won't get more than a talking-to, but it'll be a thrashing for me. I'm not likely to be careless. Now persuade your friend to pretend the lady's his.

CLINIA: I'm quite ready. As things are, I've no choice.

CLITIPHO: And I'll love you for it as you deserve.

CLINIA: But be careful *she* doesn't slip up.

SYRUS: She's been well drilled in the part.

CLITIPHO: I simply can't understand how you found it so easy to persuade her. She's said no to all sorts of people.

SYRUS: I caught her at the right moment, always the first essential. In fact I found her with an officer who was pitifully begging her for a single night, and she was handling him in her artful way so as to inflame his desire by her refusal, and at the same time keep in your own good graces. But do watch your step, sir, and don't wreck everything by being careless. You know what a sharp eye your father has for such things, and I know you and how you can let yourself go. Double meanings, side-glances, clearing your throat, sighing and coughing and laughing – none of that.

CLITIPHO: You'll be proud of me.

SYRUS [*looking along the road*]: Careful, please.

CLITIPHO: Even you will be surprised.

SYRUS: How quickly the women have caught up!

CLITIPHO: Where are they? [*struggling to free himself from* SYRUS' *grasp*] Why are you stopping me?

SYRUS: She's not yours now.

CLITIPHO: I know, when my father's there, but until then –

SYRUS: It makes no difference.

CLITIPHO: Let me go!

SYRUS: No, I won't.

CLITIPHO: Please, just for a minute –

SYRUS: No, you shan't.

CLITIPHO: Just one kiss –

SYRUS: If you've any sense you'll go.

CLITIPHO: All right, I'm going. What about *him*?

SYRUS: He's staying.

CLITIPHO: Lucky man!

SYRUS: Get moving!

[*He pushes* CLITIPHO *into* CHREMES' *house as an elegant young woman,* BACCHIS, *appears, right, with the girl,* ANTIPHILA, *followed by maids and servants with baggage.*]

BACCHIS [*rather condescending and consciously refined*]: My dear Antiphila, I congratulate you. You really have been fortunate, I think, in seeing that your morals match your beauty. Heaven knows I'm not surprised that everyone wants to make you his own, for your conversation has given me a clear idea of your character. When I think of your way of life and that of those like you who keep the vulgar crowd at a distance, I don't wonder that you are as you are and the rest of us are so different. Your virtue is a positive asset; which the men we deal with simply don't allow. It's only our looks which attract lovers to wait on us, and when these fade they take their attentions elsewhere; and if meanwhile we've made no provision for the future, we're left to a solitary life. You and your kind have only to make up your minds to spend your lives with the husbands whose characters most resemble your own, and at once they're devoted to you; with the happy result that you are truly bound together, so that your love is untouched by any misfortune.

ANTIPHILA: I can't answer for the others, but I know I've always done my best to make his interests my own.

CLINIA [unseen by ANTIPHILA]: Antiphila, my darling, nothing but you brought me back home today – for all my hardships while I was away were easy to bear except our separation.

SYRUS: I believe you.

CLINIA: Syrus, I can hardly bear it. Oh the pain of not being able to enjoy her to my heart's desire!

SYRUS: You're nowhere near that, from what I've seen of your father's attitude; he'll make life difficult for you for a long time yet.

BACCHIS: Who is that young man staring at us?

ANTIPHILA [overcome]: Oh, hold me, please.

BACCHIS: My dear girl, what's the matter?

ANTIPHILA: I can't bear it, it's too much . . .

BACCHIS: Antiphila, can't you speak? What is it?

ANTIPHILA: Is that really my Clinia?

BACCHIS: Who? Where?

CLINIA [running to catch her in his arms]: Dear heart . . .

ANTIPHILA: Clinia, my darling . . .

CLINIA: How are you?

ANTIPHILA: Happy, now that you're safely home.

CLINIA: Is it really you, Antiphila? Oh, I've longed for you with all my heart.

SYRUS [edging them towards CHREMES' house]: Go in, please. The master's been expecting you for ages.★

[They all go in. The stage is left empty to indicate passage of time. When CHREMES comes out of his house again, it is next morning.]

CHREMES: Dawn's breaking, so I think I might knock at my

★Presumably for the party mentioned on p. 89.

neighbour's door and be the first with the news that his son has returned. I believe the boy would rather I didn't, but when I see how his unhappy father is torturing himself over his son's departure, why should I deny him this unexpected joy, especially when the boy is in no danger from the disclosure? I can't do it; I shall help the old man in what way I can. I see my own son devoting himself to his friend, who's a lad of his own age, acting as his ally in all his affairs, so it's only right that we old people should support each other.

[MENEDEMUS *comes out of his house, talking to himself.*]

MENEDEMUS: Either I was born with a remarkable disposition for misery, or else there's no truth in the popular saying that time is the healer of man's suffering. In my case what I suffer for my son increases day by day, and the longer he's away the more I miss him and long for his return.

CHREMES: Why, here he is. I'll go and speak to him. Good morning, Menedemus; I've news for you which I know you are longing to hear.

MENEDEMUS: Chremes! Can you have heard anything about my son?

CHREMES: He is alive and well.

MENEDEMUS: Where is he, please?

CHREMES: In my house.

MENEDEMUS [*overwhelmed*]: My son, did you say?

CHREMES: Yes, your son.

MENEDEMUS: He's here?

CHREMES: He is indeed.

MENEDEMUS: My Clinia has come?

CHREMES: So I said.

MENEDEMUS [*taking* CHREMES *by the arm*]: Come along, please take me to him.

CHREMES: He doesn't want you to know he's back, and he's trying to keep out of your sight. He knows he did wrong, and that makes him fear that your old severity may even have increased.

MENEDEMUS: Didn't you tell him about me?

CHREMES: No, I didn't.

MENEDEMUS: Why not?

CHREMES: Because the worst thing you can do, in your own interests and in his, is to be seen in such a subdued and compliant state of mind.

MENEDEMUS: I can't help it. I've played the heavy father long enough.

CHREMES: You always run to extremes, Menedemus, one way or the other. Either you're too lavish with your money or else you're too strict, and you'll make yourself misunderstood as much by what you propose to do now as you did before. Formerly, sooner than allow your son to frequent a young woman who was content at the time with little and grateful for everything, you frightened him out of the house. She was then forced against her inclinations to make a living in the usual way. Today when she can only be kept at vast expense,* you're all eagerness to give him anything. Just let me tell you how well she's equipped now for spreading destruction. In the first place, she's brought about a dozen maids with her, each one of them laden with her dresses and jewels; she might have a foreign viceroy for a lover, but he'd never be able to meet her expenses, and you certainly can't.

MENEDEMUS [*not really listening*]: Is she in your house?

CHREMES: Isn't she! I ought to know, for last night I provided dinner for her and her companions. Another meal like that

*Chremes has been told that *Bacchis* is Clinia's mistress.

would ruin me. Apart from everything else, there's all the wine she's wasted with tasting and spitting: 'This wine's too rough, Father,' she'd say; 'have you nothing milder to offer?' I opened every jar and cask I had, kept everyone on the jump – and that's only one night. What's going to become of you, do you think, when she's continually eating you out of house and home? I'm sorry for your savings, Menedemus, God knows.

MENEDEMUS: Let him do what he likes – take, spend, squander. I'm determined to accept anything, as long as I can keep him at home.

CHREMES: Well, if you've really made up your mind, I think the important thing is that he shouldn't guess that you know the truth but are willing to keep him supplied.

MENEDEMUS: What am I to do?

CHREMES: Anything rather than what you're proposing. Pay out through someone else, let yourself be duped by his man's tricks – that's something I've already spotted: they're at it already, plotting on the sly. Syrus and that lad of yours are whispering with their heads together and passing on their schemes to the young men, and you'd do better to lose a thousand on my plan than a hundred on theirs. It's no longer a question of money, but the problem of how to give it to the boy with the minimum of risk. If he once has an inkling of your state of mind and sees that you'd throw away your life and all you have rather than lose him, you'll have opened the floodgates for dissipation, and farewell to any future pleasure in life! The fact is that all of us deteriorate when restrictions are removed. He'll fancy whatever comes into his head without a thought of right or wrong, and go straight for it. You won't be able to endure the ruin of your fortune *and* your son. But on the other hand, if you cut off supplies altogether he'll turn at once to what he thinks gives him most hold over you; he'll threaten to leave you on the spot.

MENEDEMUS [*doubtfully*]: I suppose that's true ... yes, you must be right.

CHREMES: Believe me, I didn't sleep a wink all last night for thinking how I could restore your son to you.

MENEDEMUS: Give me your hand, Chremes. Carry on, please, as you are doing.

CHREMES: I'm ready.

MENEDEMUS: Do you know what I'd like you to do now?

CHREMES: Tell me.

MENEDEMUS: As you've noticed that they are planning to trick me, try to hurry them up. I can't wait to give my boy what he wants and set eyes on him in person.

CHREMES: I'll do my best. There's just a small matter delaying me; our neighbours Simus and Crito are involved in a boundary dispute, and have asked me to arbitrate. I'd promised to see to this, but I'll go and tell them it can't be today. I'll be back in a minute.

MENEDEMUS: Please do. [CHREMES *goes off, right.*] Heavens above, how true it is that nature has equipped us all to judge another man's affairs better than our own! Is it because in our own case we are blinded by extremes of joy or sorrow? How much wiser this man is on my behalf than I am for myself.

[CHREMES *returns.*]

CHREMES: I've excused myself, and now I'm free to give you my assistance. I must catch Syrus and tell him what we want of him. [*His door is heard opening.*] Here's someone coming out; you go home, Menedemus, or they'll see that we are working together.

[MENEDEMUS *goes into his house.* SYRUS *comes out, talking to himself.*]

SYRUS: Go on, run round in circles, but you've got to find that money somehow. You must set a trap for the old man.

CHREMES [*aside*]: You see I was right about their plans. I suppose Clinia's man is too slow for the job, so they've handed it over to this fellow of mine.

SYRUS: Who's that? Oh, how frightful! Could he have heard?

CHREMES: Syrus!

SYRUS [*makes some inarticulate response*]

CHREMES: What's the matter with you?

SYRUS [*trying to gain time*]: Oh I'm all right, sir, only I'm surprised to see you out so early, after all you drank last night.

CHREMES [*stiffly*]: Nothing out of the ordinary.

SYRUS: Don't you think so, sir? Well, it looked to me like what they call life in the old dog yet.

CHREMES [*snorts*]

SYRUS: Attractive young person, isn't she, sir? Witty too.

CHREMES: No doubt she is.

SYRUS: You thought so too, sir? Marvellous figure as well.

CHREMES: Not bad.

SYRUS: Not like the girls were in your time, of course, sir, but quite good for today. No wonder Clinia's crazy about her. But he's got a mean old miser for a father in our neighbour here – do you know him? Rolling in money, and yet his son ran away from home because he hadn't a penny. It's quite true; had you heard?

CHREMES: Of course I have. Hard labour at the mill is what he deserves!

SYRUS [*puzzled*]: Who, sir?

CHREMES: Young Clinia's servant, of course . . .

SYRUS [*aside*]: That gave you a nasty fright, Syrus.

CHREMES: . . . who allowed that to happen.

SYRUS: What could he do?

CHREMES: Don't ask silly questions. He could have found some way out, devised some scheme to produce the means for the boy to give what he wanted to his mistress and to save that tiresome old father in spite of himself.

SYRUS: You're joking, sir.

CHREMES: That is what he should have done.

SYRUS: Tell me, sir, do you approve of servants' deceiving their masters?

CHREMES: Yes, on occasion, I do.

SYRUS: Quite right too!

CHREMES: It's often the solution for serious trouble. In this case, an only son would have stayed at home.

SYRUS [aside]: I can't tell whether he's joking or in earnest. Anyway, it encourages me to take advantage of it.

CHREMES: What's the fellow waiting for now, Syrus? Is he waiting till the son goes off again because he can't meet that young woman's expenses? Why can't he think up some trick to play on the old father?

SYRUS: He's not very bright, sir.

CHREMES: Then you ought to help him, for the young man's sake.

SYRUS [eagerly]: I can easily do so, if you give the word, sir. I know a bit about how these things are generally done –

CHREMES: So much the better.

SYRUS: Of course it's against my principles to tell lies . . .

CHREMES: You see to it, then.

SYRUS: Only do remember all this, sir, should it ever happen that your own son does something of this kind, human nature being what it is.

CHREMES: The situation won't arise, I hope.

SYRUS: I'm sure I hope so too, sir, and I don't mean to suggest
I've noticed anything about him at present. But if ever . . .
don't you . . . As you see, he's young. . . . [*Eagerly*] anyway, if it comes to that, sir, I'd be able to handle you in
grand style.

CHREMES [*drily*]: We'll see what's needed when the occasion
arises. Meanwhile, attend to the business in hand.

[*He goes into his house.*]

SYRUS: Never in my life have I heard my master speak more
to the point! Nor could I have believed I'd be allowed to
make trouble without paying for it! Now who's coming
out?

[CHREMES *bursts out again, dragging* CLITIPHO.]

CHREMES: What on earth do you think you are doing? Can
you explain your conduct? Is this the way to behave?

CLITIPHO [*sulkily*]: What have I done?

CHREMES: Didn't I just see you putting your hand down the
front of that woman's dress?

SYRUS [*aside*]: That's finished me; I'm done for.

CLITIPHO: What, me?

CHREMES: I saw you with my own eyes, don't deny it. Clinia
has done nothing to deserve such disgraceful treatment;
you should keep your hands to yourself. It's grossly insulting
to your friend to receive him in your own house and then
make advances to his mistress. And yesterday, when you
were drinking, you were positively indecent –

SYRUS: That's a fact.

CHREMES: – and offensive. God help me, I dreaded to think
how it would end. I know very well what lovers are, and
how they take offence in a way you might not expect.

CLITIPHO: But he trusts me not to do anything like that,
Father.

CHREMES: Maybe, but at least you could take yourself out of their sight for a while. Love leads to a lot of things where your presence would only be a hindrance. I know how I should feel, for none of my friends is the sort of man I'd dare to tell all my secrets. With one my pride stops me, with another I'm ashamed for what I've done, not wanting to look a fool or a hot-head, and you may be sure he feels the same. Our duty is to try to find out how and when we can best fall in with his wishes.

SYRUS [joining them]: What's this I hear?

CLITIPHO: Oh, damn it all!

SYRUS [to CLITIPHO, in scandalized tones]: Is this how you carry out my instructions, sir? Do you call that the self-restraint proper to an honourable man?

CLITIPHO: Be quiet, can't you.

SYRUS: A nice way to behave.

CLITIPHO: I'm sorry, Syrus.

SYRUS: I dare say you are, and so you should be. I'm very much upset.

CLITIPHO: You'll be the death of me, I swear.

SYRUS: I'm only speaking the truth, as I see it.

CLITIPHO [to CHREMES]: Can't I go anywhere near that couple?

CHREMES: Have you more than one way of going near them?

SYRUS [aside]: It's hopeless. He'll give himself away before I've had a chance to get the money. [To CHREMES] I don't profess to be clever, sir, but would you be willing to listen to me?

CHREMES: What shall I do?

SYRUS: Tell him to go off somewhere.

CLITIPHO: Where to?

SYRUS: Anywhere you like, only leave them to themselves. You go for a walk.

CLITIPHO: *Where* shall I go for a walk?

SYRUS: Good heavens, aren't there plenty of places? [*Pushing him off, left*] Go that way, over there, anywhere.

CHREMES: He's quite right. I say the same.

CLITIPHO [*calling back as he goes*]: To hell with you, Syrus, pushing me off like this!

SYRUS [*laughing*]: Then keep your hands to yourself next time! [CLITIPHO *goes.*] Do you really say the same, sir? He needs watching, and all the correction and guidance you can give him, or I don't know what he'll do one day, do you, sir?

CHREMES [*shortly*]: I'll see to that.

SYRUS: Yes, sir, you're the one who'll have to look after him now.

CHREMES: I intend to.

SYRUS: You will if you're wise, for he takes less and less notice of me.

CHREMES: And what have *you* been doing? Have you done anything about what I spoke to you about just now, or thought of anything yet which would do?

SYRUS: You mean that trick,* sir? Yes, I've just thought of one.

CHREMES: Good boy. What is it?

SYRUS: I'll tell you, sir, but first things first –

CHREMES: What do you mean?

SYRUS: That's a thoroughly bad woman, sir.

CHREMES: So she seems.

SYRUS: But if you only knew! Oh, the wickedness she's plotting. There was an old woman from Corinth living here, to whom she'd lent a thousand drachmas.

*cf. ll. 545 ff.

CHREMES: What then?

SYRUS: The old woman died, leaving a young daughter in pledge to the other as security for the loan.

CHREMES: I see.

SYRUS: The girl was brought along here, in fact she's the one indoors with your wife now.

CHREMES: What then?

SYRUS: Bacchis is asking Clinia to give her the money at once, and says he can have the girl when he does. She's demanding the thousand in cash.

CHREMES: *Demanding*, did you say?

SYRUS: Well, do you doubt it? That's what it sounded like to me.

CHREMES: What do you propose to do now?

SYRUS: I'll go to Menedemus and say the girl was kidnapped from Caria, that she's well-born and rich, and if he buys her he'll do well out of it.

CHREMES: That's a mistake.

SYRUS: Why, sir?

CHREMES: I can give you Menedemus' answer myself, straight off: 'I'm not buying.' What will you do then?

SYRUS: That's the very answer I want.

CHREMES: Why?

SYRUS: It doesn't matter.

CHREMES [*mystified*]: Doesn't matter?

SYRUS: Good lord, no.

CHREMES: I wonder what you mean.

SYRUS: You'll soon find out, sir. [*Turns to go in.*]

CHREMES: Here, wait a minute! What's that noise at our door?

[*They stand aside as* CHREMES' *wife*, SOSTRATA, *and a* NURSE *come out.*]

SOSTRATA: Unless I'm much mistaken, this is the very ring I take it to be, and the one which was with my baby daughter when she was exposed.

CHREMES [*aside, to* SYRUS]: What does she mean by that?

SOSTRATA: What do you think, nurse? Isn't it the same?

NURSE: I said so the moment you showed me it.

SOSTRATA: But are you sure you looked at it properly?

NURSE: Yes, I did.

SOSTRATA: Go in at once and tell me if she's had her bath. I shall wait out here for my husband.

[*The* NURSE *goes in.*]

SYRUS: It's you she wants, sir. Find out what it's about. Something's upset her, and there must be a reason. I feel quite nervous.

CHREMES: Do you? She makes a lot of fuss about what she has to say, but it's generally a lot of nonsense.

SOSTRATA: My dear Chremes –

CHREMES [*sarcastically*]: My dear wife.

SOSTRATA: I was looking for you.

CHREMES: Tell me what you want.

SOSTRATA: First of all, let me beg you to believe that I've never ventured to act against your instructions.

CHREMES: If you want me to believe the incredible – all right, I will.

SYRUS [*aside*]: She must have done something wrong, or she wouldn't be making these excuses.

SOSTRATA: Do you remember that time when I was pregnant and you gave me strict orders not to rear the child if it was a girl?

CHREMES: Then I know what you did; you brought it up.

SYRUS [*aside*]: Exactly; which means another mistress for me and a dead loss for my master.

SOSTRATA: I did not. But there was a woman from Corinth living here, quite a decent old thing, and I gave her the baby to expose.

CHREMES: Good God, the stupidity of the woman!

SOSTRATA: Oh dear, what have I done?

CHREMES: Can't you see?

SOSTRATA: If I did wrong, Chremes, I didn't mean to.

CHREMES: One thing I'm sure about, even if you deny it: there's never any sense or meaning in anything you do. There are any number of things wrong about this. In the first place, if you had really intended to carry out my order you should have destroyed the child at once, instead of pretending it was dead while in fact you were giving it a chance to survive. But let that pass; it was pity, you'll say, a mother's love; very well. Just think whether you made proper provision for carrying out your intention! Why, you entirely abandoned your daughter to that old woman, and for all you could do she might have made a living out of the child or sold it into slavery. I suppose you thought anything would do as long as it stayed alive. How can one deal with people who have no conception of what is just or right or good? Better or worse, gain or loss, they can see only what they want to see.

SOSTRATA: I was wrong, Chremes, I admit. I'm not trying to defend myself. All I'm asking of you now, as the years have brought you wisdom and forgiveness, is that my folly shall find protection in your sense of justice.

CHREMES: I must forgive you, I suppose, for what you did, Sostrata, but my indulgence is a poor example for you in many ways. Well, whatever your reason was for introducing this subject, let's have it.

SOSTRATA: Like any other silly superstitious woman, when

I gave the baby to the woman to expose I took a ring from my finger and told her to put it out with the child. I didn't want it to die with nothing at all from us.

CHREMES: You did right there. It was a safeguard for your own conscience as well as for the child.

SOSTRATA [*showing him a ring*]: This is the ring.

CHREMES: Where did you get it from?

SOSTRATA: The girl who came here with Bacchis –

SYRUS [*lets out a cry of astonishment*]

CHREMES: What has she to say?

SOSTRATA: – gave it to me to look after while she went to have a bath. I didn't pay much attention at first, but then when I looked at it I recognized it at once and hurried out to you.

CHREMES: Have you noticed or suspected anything about the girl?

SOSTRATA: I don't know . . . You might ask her straight out where she got it from; that's something we could find out.

SYRUS [*aside*]: Damn it, things look much too hopeful for my liking.★ If it's true, this must be our girl.

CHREMES: Is the old woman still alive?

SOSTRATA: I don't know.

CHREMES: What did she say at the time?

SOSTRATA: That she'd carried out her instructions.

CHREMES: Tell me her name, so that I can make inquiries.

SOSTRATA: Philtera.

SYRUS [*aside*]: That's her! And unless a miracle happens, the girl's found, and I'm lost!

CHREMES: Come indoors with me, Sostrata.

★ If Antiphila is free-born, she cannot be security for a loan; which puts an end to Syrus' plan of getting money out of Menedemus in ll. 603 ff.

SOSTRATA: This is more than I could have hoped. I was so afraid, Chremes, that you'd be as stony-hearted now as you were then about bringing her up.

CHREMES: A man can't always be what he chooses; circumstances don't always permit. As things are now I'm anxious for a daughter; before, there was nothing I wanted less.

[*They go into their house.*]

SYRUS: Unless I'm much mistaken, disaster's waiting for me round the corner. This has put me and my plans in a very tight place, unless I can see a way of stopping old Menedemus from discovering the girl's his son's mistress. As for my hopes about money, or my idea of being able to trick him, all that's off. It'll be a triumph if I can cover my flanks and beat a retreat. It's sheer torture to have such a morsel snatched from my lips, but what can I do? I must think up something; there's got to be a new plan of action. [*He paces about the stage.*] Nothing's too difficult for hard thinking not to find a way out. I might start this way . . . no, it won't do. What about that . . . no go either. Well, then, this . . . impossible. No, it isn't, it's perfect! Hurrah, I've a perfect plan! I do believe I'll lay hands on that fugitive cash after all.

[CLINIA *hurries out of* CHREMES' *house, in a state of high excitement.*]

CLINIA: Nothing can ever happen to me now to cast a shadow on the happiness which has dawned so bright for me! Henceforth I'll put myself entirely in my father's hands, and he'll find me as deserving as he could wish.

SYRUS: I was right; she's been recognized, if I've understood what he said. [*Coming forward*] I'm delighted to hear that things have turned out as you wanted, sir.

CLINIA: My dear Syrus, have you heard?

SYRUS: Of course. I was in on it all the time.

CLINIA: Did you ever know anyone have such luck?

SYRUS: No one.

CLINIA: And I swear to heaven I'm not so happy just on my own account – it's for her too. I know she deserves every mark of respect.

SYRUS: I'm sure she does. But now it's your turn to listen to what I've got to say. We must make sure that your friend's affairs are safely settled too, and his old father doesn't hear about his mistress Bacchis.

CLINIA [*taking no notice*]: O Gods above!

SYRUS: Do be quiet.

CLINIA: My Antiphila will marry me!

SYRUS: *Must* you interrupt?

CLINIA [*hugging him*]: What am I to do? Syrus, dear man, I'm so happy; bear with me.

SYRUS: That's exactly what I am doing.

CLINIA: We've won a place among the gods!

SYRUS [*crossly*]: It seems to me I'm just wasting my time.

CLINIA: Carry on; I'm listening now.

SYRUS: But you won't next minute.

CLINIA: Yes I will.

SYRUS: What I said, sir, was that we must make sure that your friend's affairs are also safely settled. If you leave Bacchis behind when you move out of our house, my master'll find out straight away that she's Clitipho's mistress. If you take her away with you, the secret won't come out any more than it has done up to now.

CLINIA [*dismayed*]: Yes, but Syrus, nothing is more likely to stand in the way of my wedding. What sort of expression am I to wear when I approach my father? What do you suggest I'm to say?

SYRUS: It's quite simple.

CLINIA: Then what *am* I to say? What reason can I give?

SYRUS: I don't intend you to go telling a lot of lies. Be quite frank with him, and tell him the truth.

CLINIA: What!

SYRUS: I mean it. Say you love Antiphila and want to marry her, and the other girl is Clitipho's.

CLINIA [*with heavy sarcasm*]: A very right and proper suggestion; so easy to carry out too. And I suppose you'd also like me to beg my father to keep it from your master?

SYRUS: On the contrary, he can tell the whole story, straight out.

CLINIA: You must be mad or drunk. You're the one who'll ruin Clitipho, that's obvious. What's 'safely settled' for him in that, pray?

SYRUS: That's my prize plan, the one I'm really proud of! [*Drawing himself up*] It reveals in me such a powerful force of ingenuity that I can deceive the pair of them simply by telling the truth! Don't you see – when my old master hears from your father that Bacchis is his son's mistress, he simply won't believe it.

CLINIA: Yes, but this plan of yours will once again destroy all my hopes of marriage. So long as your master thinks Bacchis is *my* mistress, he won't trust me with his daughter. Maybe you're not interested in what becomes of me, so long as you can look after Clitipho.

SYRUS: Damn it all, sir, are you suggesting that I want this pretence kept up for ever? It's only for one day, while I can get the money out of him, that's all; not a minute more.

CLINIA: But do you think that gives you enough time? And what are we to do if his father finds out the truth?

SYRUS: Well, all I can say is that there are people who say 'what if the sky falls?'

CLINIA: I'm afraid of what I've got to do.

SYRUS: No need to be afraid; you can extricate yourself whenever you like, simply by publishing the facts.

CLINIA [*reluctantly*]: All right then. Bring Bacchis over to us.

SYRUS [*as* CHREMES' *door opens*]: Luckily she's coming out herself.

> [BACCHIS *comes out, in a very bad temper, with her maid; the others stand back.*]

BACCHIS: Damn Syrus for his impudence, bringing me here with his promises of a thousand drachmas! If he's deceived me this time he'll ask and ask in future, but his errand will be in vain. Or else I'll say I'll come and fix a time, and then when he's taken back the message and raised Clitipho's hopes I can play the deceiver and not turn up, and Syrus' back shall smart for it.

CLINIA [*to* SYRUS]: That's a nice promise to make you.

SYRUS: And do you think she's joking? She'll do it if I don't look out.

BACCHIS [*aside*]: They're asleep. I'll make them sit up. [*Aloud*] Phrygia, my dear, did you hear which house it was that man told us was Charinus's?

PHRYGIA: Yes, I did.

BACCHIS: Was it the next one on the right, after this farm?

PHRYGIA: That's what I remember.

BACCHIS: Just run on ahead. My captain's celebrating the holiday with him –

SYRUS: Now what's she up to?

BACCHIS: – and you can tell him I'm here, detained against my will, but somehow I'll manage to outwit these people and come.

SYRUS: That'll finish me. Stop, Bacchis, stop! Where are you sending her please? Tell her to stop.

BACCHIS: Go on.

[PHRYGIA *starts to move off, left.*]

SYRUS: But the money's there, waiting for you.

BACCHIS: Well then, I'll stay.

[PHRYGIA *returns.*]

SYRUS: You'll have it at once.

BACCHIS [*graciously*]: At your convenience. I'm not pressing you.

SYRUS: But have you heard this, if you please –

BACCHIS: What?

SYRUS: You're to move over to Menedemus's at once and take all the maids with you.

BACCHIS: What on earth do you mean by that, you rascal?

SYRUS: Well, I'm ... I'm coining money, you might say, to give you.

BACCHIS: Do you think I'm a proper object for your jokes?

SYRUS: I'm quite serious.

BACCHIS: In that case, have we any more to say to each other?

SYRUS: No, I was only paying you your due.

BACCHIS: Let us go, then.

SYRUS: Come this way. [*He knocks at* MENEDEMUS' *door.*] Hi, Dromo!

[DROMO *comes out.*]

DROMO: Who's calling me?

SYRUS: It's me, Syrus.

DROMO: What's the matter?

SYRUS: Take all Bacchis' maids across to your place, and look sharp.

DROMO: What for?

SYRUS: Don't ask. See that they take away what they brought with them. [DROMO *goes into* CHREMES' *house and soon reappears with the maids and all the luggage.*] My old master'll hope to cut down his expenses by this exodus, but he little knows how much this small gain is going to cost him! Dromo, if you're wise, you'll forget about all this.

DROMO: You can count me dumb.

[*He shepherds all the women into* MENEDEMUS' *house. Almost at once* CHREMES *comes out.*]

CHREMES: God knows I'm sorry for Menedemus and his wretched lot! Fancy having to support that female and all her set-up! I know he's been so anxious to see his son again that he won't notice it for the next few days, but once he realizes the huge expenses he'll have in his home every day, and no end to them, he'll be only too glad to see the back of him again. Ah, here's Syrus; that's luck.

SYRUS [*aside*]: Now for it!

CHREMES: Syrus!

SYRUS [*with exaggerated pleasure*]: Well I never!

CHREMES: What do you mean?

SYRUS: I've been hoping to run into you for ages, sir.

CHREMES: You look as though you'd already fixed up something with our neighbour.

SYRUS: In the matter we were just . . . Yes, sir, no sooner said than done.

CHREMES: Upon your honour?

SYRUS: Upon my honour, sir.

CHREMES [*genially*]: You'll have to have a pat on the head for that, Syrus. Come over here. I'll do you a good turn for this, and gladly.

SYRUS: Ah, if you only knew the bright idea I had!

CHREMES [*laughing*]: Now, now, are you boasting that everything went according to plan?

SYRUS: Certainly not, sir, I was only telling the truth.

CHREMES: Well then, tell it.

SYRUS: Clinia has told his father that this woman Bacchis is your Clitipho's mistress, and that he's only brought her with him to prevent your finding out.

CHREMES [*laughing*]: Good.

SYRUS: What do you think of that!

CHREMES: Excellent, I say.

SYRUS [*aside*]: Ah, if you only knew . . . But let me tell you the rest of the trick. Clinia is also pretending that he's seen your daughter and fallen in love with her beauty at first sight, and wants to make her his wife.

CHREMES: My newly discovered daughter?

SYRUS: Yes; and he'll get his father to ask for her.

CHREMES: What's all this about, Syrus? I don't quite get that.

SYRUS: You're a bit slow, sir.

CHREMES: Perhaps I am.

SYRUS: Clinia'll be given money for the *wedding*, for jewels and dresses and so on – got it now?

CHREMES: You mean, to buy them?

SYRUS: Yes, of course.

CHREMES [*still obtuse*]: But I'm not giving him nor promising him my daughter.

SYRUS: Won't you, sir? Why not?

CHREMES: Why not? What a question! A man who . . .

SYRUS [*hastily*]: Yes, yes, of course. I wasn't suggesting anything *permanent*, sir, only that you should *pretend* to let him have her.

CHREMES: I'm not given to pretence of that sort. Carry on with your concoctions, but don't mix me up in them. Am I likely to promise her to a man I've no intention of giving her to?

SYRUS: I just thought you might.

CHREMES: Certainly not.

SYRUS [*crestfallen*]: It was such a bright idea. And I only started on it because you'd been badgering me so long to do something.

CHREMES: I dare say.

SYRUS: Anyway, your attitude is quite correct and proper, sir. I accept that.

CHREMES: But I'm still very anxious for you to make a success of this, only by some other way.

SYRUS: All right, we must think of something else. But there's still that money which I told you was owed to Bacchis on account of your daughter.* It's got to be paid at once, and I'm sure you're not one to make excuses that it's nothing to do with you, because you never saw the money or gave any instructions, and the old woman had no power to pledge your daughter without your consent. It's a true saying that 'strictest law means greatest hardship'.

CHREMES: I shan't do anything like that.

SYRUS: No, sir, others may, but not you; you're well known to be well set up in a nice little fortune.

CHREMES: In fact I shall take the money to her now myself.

SYRUS [*hastily*]: I shouldn't do that, sir; tell your son to take it.

CHREMES: Why?

SYRUS: Because the suspicion of being her lover has been transferred to *him*.

CHREMES: What's that got to do with it?

SYRUS: It'll seem more plausible if he's the one to hand over the money; and it'll also make it easier for me to carry out what I've in mind. [*Looking along the road, left*] Why, here he comes. You go in, sir, and fetch the money.

CHREMES: I will.

* The supposed loan for which Antiphila was said to be security. See ll. 600 ff.

[He goes into his house as CLITIPHO *walks wearily on, left.]*

CLITIPHO: Anything easy seems difficult when you don't want to do it. This wasn't really a tiring walk but I'm exhausted. The one thing I dread at the moment is to be pushed off again, just to make me miserable and keep me away from Bacchis. [*He sees* SYRUS.] May all the gods in heaven confound you, Syrus, with your schemes and inventions! You're always thinking up things like this to make my life a misery.

SYRUS: Go to hell, can't you, where you belong. You nearly did for me altogether, the liberties you take.*

CLITIPHO: My God, I wish I had done; it's what you deserved!

SYRUS: *How* did I deserve it? I'm glad you told me that *before* you got your hands on the money I was going to give you.

CLITIPHO: What do you want me to say? You went off and fetched my mistress, and then I wasn't allowed to touch her.

SYRUS: I'm not angry with you now. But do you know where your Bacchis is at the present moment?

CLITIPHO: In our house.

SYRUS: No.

CLITIPHO: Where is she then?

SYRUS: At Clinia's.

CLITIPHO [*horrified*]: What!

SYRUS: Cheer up. You're going to take her the money you promised her.

CLITIPHO: Nonsense. Where can I get it from?

SYRUS: Your father.

CLITIPHO: I suppose that's your idea of a joke.

SYRUS: Events will show.

*Clitipho's behaviour with Bacchis, noticed by Chremes in ll. 562 ff.

CLITIPHO: Then I'm a lucky man! [*Seizing him*] Syrus, I adore you!

SYRUS: Here's your father coming out. Be careful not to show surprise at any reason for this. Humour him at the right moment, do what he says, say as little as possible.

[CHREMES *comes out, with money.*]

CHREMES: Where's Clitipho?

SYRUS [*whispers*]: Say 'here I am!'

CLITIPHO: Here I am, father.

CHREMES: How much have you told him?

SYRUS: Pretty well everything.

CHREMES: Take this money then, and give it to your girl-friend.

[CLITIPHO *is thunderstruck.*]

SYRUS: Go on, don't stand there like a log; take it.

CLITIPHO: All right, give it to me.

SYRUS: Come along with me, and hurry up. You wait here, sir, until we come out. There's nothing to keep us there long.

[*He takes* CLITIPHO *into* MENEDEMUS' *house.*]

CHREMES: That means that my daughter has already cost me a thousand drachmas, which I reckon as covering her maintenance; now there'll be another thousand for a trousseau, and then a further twelve thousand for her dowry. How many unjust and unnatural demands convention makes on us! And now I have to lay everything aside and look for someone to whom I can hand over my hard-earned wealth.

[MENEDEMUS *comes out, speaking to* CLINIA *within.*]

MENEDEMUS: I count myself the happiest man in the whole world, Clinia, now that I see you restored to your senses.*

CHREMES [*aside*]: That's where he's wrong!

*Clinia has told his father that Bacchis is really Clitipho's mistress.

MENEDEMUS: Why, Chremes, I was looking for you. Please do all you can to bring happiness to my son, myself and all of us!

CHREMES: What do you want me to do?

MENEDEMUS: Today you have recognized a daughter –

CHREMES: Yes, what of it?

MENEDEMUS: Clinia wants her for his wife.

CHREMES: What sort of a man are you, I wonder?

MENEDEMUS: What do you mean?

CHREMES: Have you already forgotten our conversation about that trick – which was to be a way of getting money out of you?*

MENEDEMUS: I remember.

CHREMES: This is the trick.

MENEDEMUS: What do you say, Chremes? Am I mistaken? Is this what they've done? Oh, it's the end of all my high hopes! But that woman in my house is Clitipho's mistress, not Clinia's; they told me so.

CHREMES: And you believe it all. They also tell you Clinia wants to marry simply so that once you've arranged the wedding you'll give him money to buy jewels and dresses and everything else that's needed.

MENEDEMUS [*after a shocked pause*]: Yes, that must be right. And it'll all go to his mistress?

CHREMES: Of course it will.

MENEDEMUS [*sighing*]: So all my rejoicing was in vain. But even now I'd rather lose anything than my boy. What answer can I take back from you, Chremes, so that he won't know I know and be angry with me?

CHREMES: *Angry*? Really, Menedemus, you're much too good to him.

*ll. 470–5.

MENEDEMUS: Don't try to change me, Chremes. I've chosen my course, help me to carry it through to the end.

CHREMES: Tell him you met me and discussed the marriage.

MENEDEMUS: I will. And then?

CHREMES: Tell him I was quite agreeable, and approved of him as a son-in-law. If you like, you can also say that I've agreed with you to let him have her.

MENEDEMUS: That's exactly what I wanted!

CHREMES [*scornfully*]: Then he'll be all the quicker with his demands on you, and you can give him the money as soon as possible: which is your main object.

MENEDEMUS: Yes it is.

CHREMES: As far as I can see, you'll soon be sick of the whole business. But in any event, if you're wise you'll be cautious and pay out small sums.

MENEDEMUS: All right.

CHREMES: Go in then, and find out how much he asks for. I shall be at home if you need me.

MENEDEMUS: I *shall* need you, for I want to keep you informed of what I do.

[*They both go into their houses, and there is a short interval, after which* MENEDEMUS *comes out again, looking happier, as he has learned the truth.*]

MENEDEMUS: I know I'm not as bright as some and not so quick in the uptake, but that guide and mentor of mine, that self-appointed manager of my affairs Chremes outdoes me by a long way. Any of the usual epithets for the stupid suit me – blockhead, numskull, nit-wit, ass – but what can you say about him? His stupidity's beyond description.

[CHREMES *comes out, talking back to* SOSTRATA *within.*]

CHREMES: For heaven's sake, woman, stop bothering the

gods with thanks for the discovery of your daughter; unless you think they take after you and can't grasp anything unless it's repeated a hundred times. Meanwhile, what's that son of ours doing all this time, waiting about with Syrus?

MENEDEMUS: Who do you say is waiting about, Chremes?

CHREMES: Oh, Menedemus, there you are. Have you told Clinia what I said?

MENEDEMUS: Every word.

CHREMES: What did he say?

MENEDEMUS: He showed his delight at once, like anyone who wants to marry.

CHREMES [laughs]

MENEDEMUS: What are you laughing at?

CHREMES: I just thought of Syrus and his tricks.

MENEDEMUS: In what way?

CHREMES: He can make up people's faces, the rascal!

MENEDEMUS: You mean my son's delight was simply put on?

CHREMES: Of course.

MENEDEMUS [humouring him]: The same thing occurred to me.

CHREMES: Just one of his usual tricks!

MENEDEMUS [with irony]: As you'll soon know for certain when you hear more.

CHREMES: Really?

MENEDEMUS: Just you listen –

CHREMES: Wait a bit, I'd like to know first what it's cost you so far. When you told your son he could have my daughter, I expect Dromo put in a word about all the dresses and jewels and maids they'd need for the bride, in order to get some money out of you.

MENEDEMUS: No.

CHREMES: What! He didn't?

MENEDEMUS: No, I say.

CHREMES: Then didn't your son?

MENEDEMUS: Not a word of that, Chremes. The one thing he insisted on was that the wedding should take place today.

CHREMES: That's amazing. What about Syrus? Had *he* nothing to say?

MENEDEMUS: Nothing.

CHREMES: I can't think why.

MENEDEMUS [*with satisfaction*]: Personally, I find *that* amazing, when you're so well informed about other things. But that Syrus of yours certainly did an amazingly good job of make-up on *your* son; there's not the slightest reason to suspect now that Bacchis is *Clinia's* mistress.

CHREMES: Clitipho! What's he doing?

MENEDEMUS: To say nothing of kisses in each other's arms, I don't count those –

CHREMES: How can pretence go further?

MENEDEMUS [*cryptically*]: Aha!

CHREMES: What do you mean?

MENEDEMUS: Just listen. I've a room right at the back of the house. A bed was taken in and made up.

CHREMES: What happened then?

MENEDEMUS: In darted Clitipho, like a flash.

CHREMES: Alone?

MENEDEMUS: Alone.

CHREMES: I don't like the sound of this . . .

MENEDEMUS: Bacchis followed at once –

CHREMES: Alone?

MENEDEMUS: Alone.

CHREMES: Damn!

MENEDEMUS: Once inside, they shut the door . . .

CHREMES: Oh . . . And did Clinia see this?

MENEDEMUS: Of course. He was there, with me.

CHREMES: So Bacchis is my son's mistress! Oh Menedemus, I'm ruined.

MENEDEMUS: Why?

CHREMES: My household can scarcely stand it ten days.

MENEDEMUS [*enjoying himself*]: Why, are you so alarmed because he's trying to help his friend?

CHREMES: It's his *girl*-friend that's worrying me.

MENEDEMUS: If that's what she is.

CHREMES: Can you doubt it? Do you suppose anyone could be so free-and-easy as to allow his mistress ... under his nose ...

MENEDEMUS [*laughing*]: Well, why not? It might be all part of the trick against *me*.

CHREMES: You're laughing at me, and no wonder. I'm furious with myself now. There were so many indications which could have pointed the way to the truth if I hadn't been so obtuse. The things I saw! What a fool I am! But they shan't get away with this while I'm alive. I'll –

MENEDEMUS: Have you no self-control? No regard for yourself? Am I not warning enough for you?

CHREMES: I'm beside myself with rage.

MENEDEMUS: How can you talk like that! You ought to be ashamed to give advice to others and be reasonable abroad when you can't help yourself at home.

CHREMES: What am I to do?

MENEDEMUS: What you kept telling me I failed to do. Make the boy feel that you are a true father, one he dare trust with everything, to whom he can make his requests and demands; otherwise he'll look for help elsewhere and abandon you.

CHREMES: No. I would rather he went off to the ends of the earth than stayed here to reduce his father to beggary by his misdeeds. For if I continue to meet his expenses, Menedemus, I'll be the one who has to make a living by the mattock.

MENEDEMUS: What trouble you'll create for yourself if you're not careful! You'll let him see you're unsympathetic, then you'll forgive him later all the same and get no thanks for it.

CHREMES: You've no idea what I feel . . .

MENEDEMUS: Very well, have it your own way. And now, what about my request that your daughter should marry my son? Unless, of course, there's anything you'd like better.

CHREMES: No, no, I've no objection to the match or the boy's connexions.

MENEDEMUS: What dowry shall I tell him you mentioned? [*There is an uncomfortable pause.*] Can't you speak?

CHREMES [*lost in thought*]: Dowry?

MENEDEMUS: That's what I said.

CHREMES: Well. . . .

MENEDEMUS: Don't worry, Chremes, if it's not much; the dowry doesn't matter to us.

CHREMES [*slowly*]: I was thinking that twelve thousand drachmas was about right for my means; but if you want to save me and my fortune *and* my son, you can say that the dowry I'm giving her is everything I have.

MENEDEMUS: Why are you doing this?

CHREMES: Pretend to be astonished, and at the same time ask Clitipho why he thinks I'm doing it.

MENEDEMUS: I've no idea why.

CHREMES: Haven't you? Well, at the moment he's abandoning himself to loose living and extravagance. I want to curb his high spirits – he won't know where to turn when I've finished with him.

MENEDEMUS: What *are* you up to?

CHREMES: Never mind, just let me go my own way in this matter.

MENEDEMUS: All right, if that's what you want.

CHREMES: Yes, I do.

MENEDEMUS: Very well.

CHREMES: Tell Clinia to get ready to fetch his wife. I'll silence *my* son with a good talking-to, the proper way to deal with children. As for Syrus –

MENEDEMUS: What about him?

CHREMES: Sure as I live, I'll give him such a dressing-down, such a beating that he'll remember me to the end of his days – thinking he could have his fun making a laughing-stock out of *me*! The sort of thing he wouldn't dare to try out on a helpless widow!

[*During this short speech* MENEDEMUS *has gone into his house;* CHREMES *paces up and down, fuming, until he returns with* CLITIPHO *and* SYRUS.]

CLITIPHO: Is that really so, Menedemus? Has my father shed all paternal feeling for me in so short a time? What have I done? What unlucky crime have I committed? I've only done what everyone does.

MENEDEMUS: I'm just as much upset as you are, though I know it's much harder and more painful for you as the real sufferer. I can't understand it at all. I don't know what I can do except assure you of my warm sympathy.

CLITIPHO: You said my father was out here?

MENEDEMUS: There he is.

[MENEDEMUS *goes in again.*]

CHREMES: What have you to complain about, Clitipho? Whatever I've done was done to save you from yourself and your folly. When I saw you so heedless, giving first place to the pleasures of the moment and incapable of taking a longer view, I thought of a plan to keep you from beggary and make it impossible for you to lose all we have. You have only yourself to blame if I could not give you the inheritance on which you have first claim. I therefore turned to your next-of-kin, and have put everything securely in her hands. You will always find a refuge from your folly with her, Clitipho, and food and clothing and a roof over your head.

CLITIPHO [*tearfully*]: Oh dear!

CHREMES: It was better than leaving everything to you for Bacchis to lay her hands on.

SYRUS [*aside*]: Damn me for a mischief-maker! Look at the trouble I've stirred up unawares!

CLITIPHO: I wish I were dead!

CHREMES [*drily*]: You'd better learn first what it is to live. When you know that, if you've no use for life you can try dying.

SYRUS: Please, sir, may I . . .?

CHREMES: Speak.

SYRUS: But – is it safe?

CHREMES: Speak.

SYRUS: Don't you think it's all wrong of you, sir, quite crazy in fact, to visit my faults on the young master here?

CHREMES [*calmly*]: Run away, and don't interfere. No one's accusing *you*, Syrus. You needn't look for sanctuary nor anyone to beg you off.

SYRUS: I don't understand.

CHREMES: I'm not angry with you; nor with you, Clitipho; so neither of you has any right to complain about what I'm doing.

[*He walks firmly into his house and shuts the door.*]

SYRUS: Has he gone? Oh, I wanted to ask him –

CLITIPHO [*gloomily*]: What?

SYRUS: Where I was to seek my daily bread. Look how he's cast me off! *You* can go to your sister I hear.

CLITIPHO: Things have come to a pretty pass, Syrus, if I'm in danger of starving.

SYRUS: So long as there's life, there's hope –

CLITIPHO: Hope of what?

SYRUS: – that we'll have to go hungry.

CLITIPHO: How can you joke at a time like this! Haven't you any helpful suggestion?

SYRUS: Well, as a matter of fact, I have, and I was thinking about it all the time your father was talking. As far as I can see –

CLITIPHO: What?

SYRUS [*playing for time*]: It'll come to me soon . . .

CLITIPHO: What is it then?

SYRUS: Got it! I don't believe you can be their son.

CLITIPHO: What on earth do you mean, Syrus? You must be crazy.

SYRUS: Let me tell you what I've thought of, then you can judge. So long as you were their only child, their chief and sole delight, they spoilt you and gave you anything you wanted. Now that they've found a true daughter of their own, they've also found an excuse to get rid of you.

CLITIPHO [*only half-convinced*]: It seems likely . . .

SYRUS: Do you suppose it was really your bad behaviour which annoyed your father?

CLITIPHO: No, I don't.

SYRUS: Here's another point; all mothers stand up for their sons in disgrace and always help them when their fathers are unjust, but there's nothing like that now.

CLITIPHO: You're right, Syrus. So what am I to do now?

SYRUS: Question them about your suspicions, bring the whole thing into the open. They'll soon be sorry for you if you are their son, and if you aren't, you'll find out whose son you really are.

CLITIPHO: That's good advice. I'll take it.

[*He goes into* CHREMES' *house.*]

SYRUS: A very happy thought of mine! The more genuinely he appears to have suspicions and the more he despairs, the easier it'll be for him to dictate peace to his father on his own terms. I wouldn't be surprised if he married in the end, though there'll be small thanks for Syrus if he does! Now what's that? Master's coming out; I'm off. After what's happened I wonder he didn't order me to be packed off at once. I'll go across to Menedemus and get him to intercede for me; I don't trust our old man.

[*He goes into* MENEDEMUS' *house;* CHREMES *and* SOS-TRATA *come out after a short interval.*]

SOSTRATA: You must be careful, Chremes, or you'll do our son an injury. I simply can't imagine how such a foolish thought could enter your head.

CHREMES: Just like a woman! I never wanted anything in my life, but you set yourself against me. But if I ask you where I'm wrong or why you behave like this, you don't know, though you remain as obstinate as ever, you stupid creature.

SOSTRATA [*indignantly*]: Do you say I don't know?

CHREMES: All right, you do know; anything rather than going all over the same ground again.

SOSTRATA: Oh, you're quite unjust! This is something so important, and you forbid me to speak.

CHREMES: I'm not stopping you; speak now; but I shall carry on just the same.

SOSTRATA: Will you?

CHREMES: Indeed I shall.

SOSTRATA: But can't you see the wrong you'll do him? He's already suspecting that he's not our son.

CHREMES: Not our son, did you say?

SOSTRATA: That's what it'll come to.

CHREMES [*sarcastically*]: And do you admit it?

SOSTRATA: For Heaven's sake, leave that for our enemies! Why ever should I admit that he's not my son when he is?

CHREMES: Why, are you afraid you can't prove he's yours whenever you like?

SOSTRATA [*puzzled*]: Because I've done this for my long-lost daughter, do you mean?

CHREMES: No, there's a much more plausible reason; he's so like you in your ways, you can easily prove he's your son. He's exactly like you, not a single fault in him which isn't the same as yours; you're the only person who could possibly be the mother of such a son. [CLITIPHO *comes out.*] Here he comes now, sunk in gloom! You've only got to look at him to guess the truth.

CLITIPHO: Mother, if there was ever a time when I brought you pleasure, and you were both glad to call me your son, remember it now, I beseech you, and take pity on my present plight. My sole desire, my only request is to hear from you who my parents were.

SOSTRATA: My son, I implore you not to get it into your head that you are someone else's child.

CLITIPHO: But it's true, isn't it?

SOSTRATA: Oh dear me, how could you ask such a question? You are as truly my son and his as I pray you may survive us both. If you love me, please don't let me ever hear you say such a thing again.

CHREMES: But if you respect my wishes, make sure I see you change your ways.

CLITIPHO: What ways?

CHREMES: I can tell you, if you want to know. You're an idle, good-for-nothing fraud, and a damned loose-living spendthrift. Believe that, and then believe you're our son.

CLITIPHO: I never thought to hear that from my father.

CHREMES: If you'd been born out of my head, as they say Minerva sprang from Jove's, it wouldn't make it any easier for me to bear the disgrace you've brought on me by your misdeeds.

SOSTRATA: Heaven preserve us from anything like that!

CHREMES [*grimly*]: I can't answer for heaven; I can only do my best for myself. You're looking for parents, and these you've got. You don't think of looking for what you haven't got – a willing spirit to obey your father and preserve what he won by honest toil. Didn't you resort to trickery to bring into my house, under my own eyes a – Oh, I'm ashamed to use such a shocking word before your mother. But you weren't ashamed to do what you did.

CLITIPHO [*aside*]: Oh God, how I hate myself now. I'm so ashamed, and I've no idea how to set about placating him.
    [MENEDEMUS *comes out of his house.*]

MENEDEMUS: Chremes is certainly too hard on the boy. It's quite inhuman, the way he torments him. So I'm coming out to make peace between them. Ah, good, there they are.

CHREMES: Well, Menedemus, why don't you send for my daughter and make sure of the dowry I offered?

SOSTRATA: My dear husband, I implore you not to do this.

CLITIPHO: Father, I implore you to forgive me.

MENEDEMUS: Take my advice, Chremes, and pardon him.

CHREMES: And make a present of my fortune to Bacchis with my eyes open? Certainly not.

MENEDEMUS: But we are here to stop that.

CLITIPHO: If you want me to stay alive, Father, you must forgive me.

SOSTRATA: Come, Chremes my dear.

MENEDEMUS: Come, Chremes, please don't be so obstinate.

CHREMES [*reluctantly*]: Very well. I see I'm not allowed to carry out my intention.

MENEDEMUS: There, now you're doing the right thing.

CHREMES: I'll forgive him on one condition: that he does what *I* think is proper for him.

CLITIPHO [*eagerly*]: Just tell me, Father, and I'll do anything.

CHREMES: You can take a wife.

CLITIPHO [*astounded*]: Father!

CHREMES: Not a word.

SOSTRATA: I'll answer for him; he'll do it.

CHREMES: Not a word from *him* yet.

CLITIPHO [*to himself*]: Oh no, no . . .

SOSTRATA: Are you hesitating, Clitipho?

CHREMES: It's for him to decide.

SOSTRATA: He'll do everything.

MENEDEMUS [*patting him on the back*]: The first plunge seems hard, when it's all new to you, but you'll find it's quite easy once you've tried it.

CLITIPHO [*with an effort*]: All right, Father, I will.

SOSTRATA: And I'll find you such a charming bride, Clitipho, it'll be easy to love her – our friend Phanocrates' daughter.

CLITIPHO [*outraged*]: That red-headed, hook-nosed girl with green eyes and a spotty face? I'm not having *her*.

CHREMES: Good gracious, how choosy he is! You'd think his mind runs on marriage.

SOSTRATA: I'll find you someone else.

CLITIPHO: No, if I must marry, I've someone in mind whom I like quite well.

CHREMES [*drily*]: Congratulations, my son.

CLITIPHO: It's our neighbour Archonides' daughter.

SOSTRATA [*eagerly*]: Oh, I like her *very* much.

CLITIPHO: There's still one thing, Father –

CHREMES: What?

CLITIPHO: I'd like you to forgive Syrus. What he did was for my sake.

CHREMES [*cheerfully*]: All right, I will.

[*They all go in.*]

PHORMIO

INTRODUCTORY NOTE

Phormio is aptly named after the character who dominates the play. There is no one quite of his stature in any other Roman comedy – he is the genuine adventurer who lives by his wits, a far more vigorous personality than any conventional sponger, such as Gnatho in *The Eunuch*, whose sole aim is to wheedle his way into a comfortable life. Phormio is called in almost in a professional capacity (much as old Demipho brings in his legal advisers) to help the two young men out of their difficulties, and he applies his ingenuity to the task of extracting money from their fathers more for the pleasure of exercising his skill than for what he may hope to get out of it himself. As Gilbert Norwood remarks, 'To all seeming Phormio conducts and administers a swindle on the principle of "art for art's sake".'

This is pure comedy of intrigue, moving as lightly and rapidly as a French farce. Phormio is always on top of every situation, and we never doubt that he will succeed; thus we are left free to concentrate on the finesse of his movements. There is no place here for the romantic touch of *The Girl from Andros*, the greater seriousness of *The Self-Tormentor* and *The Mother-in-Law*, or the subtlety of *The Brothers*, but Terence's characters always behave consistently as human beings within the framework of comic conventions, and are more than character-types. The pimp or slave-dealer Dorio, for instance, is not abused and caricatured as he would be in a comedy by Plautus; like Sannio in *The Brothers* he plays a small but plausible part as a man-of-business who quite properly stands up for his legal rights. The two elderly brothers are neatly contrasted, Chremes with his anxiety to save his reputation at all costs, and Demipho, the more positive character. His meanness and obstinate determination not to part with his money cause most of the trouble, and, in the end, precipitate Phormio's disclosure about the one thing he and Chremes are trying to conceal.

Phormio was followed very closely by Molière in *Les Fourberies de Scapin*, and one way of appreciating how it was possible for Terence to be a creative writer while using Greek models is to compare this lively comedy in its French setting with the Latin original.

PRODUCTION NOTICE

PHORMIO by Terence: performed at the Roman Games* during the curule aedileship of Lucius Postumius Albinus and Lucius Cornelius Merula.

Produced by Lucius Ambivius Turpio and Lucius Atilius of Praeneste.

Music composed by Flaccus, slave of Claudius, for unmatched pipes throughout.

Greek original *The Claimant* by Apollodorus.†

The author's fourth play, written during the consulship of Gaius Fannius and Marcus Valerius.‡

*Held annually on 4 September in honour of Jupiter.
†Apollodorus of Carystus, a writer of New Comedy in the first half of the third century B.C.
‡i.e. 161 B.C.

SYNOPSIS

Demipho, brother of Chremes, went abroad leaving his son Antipho
at Athens. Chremes had contracted a secret marriage in Lemnos and
kept a wife and daughter there. His first wife was at Athens with his
son, Phaedria, in love with a lute-player. The wife in Lemnos came
to Athens and died there, leaving only her daughter Phanium to
arrange her funeral (Chremes was away at the time). There Antipho
saw her, fell in love and married her with the aid of an adventurer,
Phormio. His father and Chremes are furious on their return and give
Phormio 3,000 drachmas to marry the girl himself; but this money is
used to buy the lute-player for Phaedria. However, Chremes recog-
nizes his daughter, and so Antipho is allowed to keep her as his wife.

AUTHOR'S PROLOGUE TO *PHORMIO*

Since the old playwright* cannot divert the author from his calling and force him to retire he is now trying to deter him from writing by use of slander. He goes on damning all his previous plays for thin dialogue and weak composition, simply because none of them contains a love-lorn youth who sees hounds pursuing a fleeing hind which begs and prays him to save her. But if he realized that on the occasion when *he* had a success with a new play the credit should really go to the producer, not himself, he would be a great deal more restrained in his insinuations. Some of you may be saying, or at least thinking, that if the old playwright had not launched the first attack, the young one would have had no one to answer and so no material for a prologue. The answer to that is that the prize of victory is open to all dramatic poets. The old playwright set out to drive the other from his profession and leave him to starve. The young one intends this to be his answer, not a further challenge. Fair words would have been answered by fair words; as things are he must realize that he is only being paid in the same coin.

For my part I shall stop talking about him, although he puts no stop to his misdeeds. Now please listen to what I have to say. I am presenting for the first time a comedy entitled *The Claimant* in Greek and *Phormio* in Latin, for the adventurer Phormio plays the leading part and directs most of the intrigue, as you will see if the author has your support. Pay attention, and give us a fair hearing in silence, so that we do not suffer the same fate as we did when the uproar drove our company from

*Luscius Lanuvinus.

the stage.* Now we are here again, thanks to the courage of
our producer and your own sense of fairness and goodwill.

*The first and second productions of *The Mother-in-Law* failed
because of the alternative attractions of boxers, tight-rope walkers and
gladiators. See the Prologue to the Third Production (*The Brothers and
Other Plays*, p. 91 ff.).

CHARACTERS

DAVOS   *a slave*

GETA   *a slave, Demipho's servant*

ANTIPHO   *a young man, son of Demipho*

PHAEDRIA   *his cousin, son of Chremes*

DEMIPHO   *an Athenian gentleman*

PHORMIO   *an adventurer*

CRATINUS

CRITO   } *Demipho's legal advisers*

HEGIO

DORIO   *a pimp*

CHREMES   *Demipho's brother*

SOPHRONA   *nurse to Phanium, Chremes' daughter*

NAUSISTRATA   *Chremes' wife*

Phanium, Chremes' daughter by his bigamous marriage in Lemnos, and Pamphila, the music-girl belonging to Dorio, do not appear

*

The scene is laid in Athens in front of the houses of Demipho, Chremes and Dorio. To the audience's right the street leads to the centre of the town, to the left to the harbour

[*The slave* DAVOS *comes on from the right carrying a bag of money.*]

DAVOS: My great friend and ally Geta came to me yesterday about a piddling little sum outstanding on an old debt of mine. I was to find the money and I did. Here it is. I hear his master's son has got married, so I suppose he's scraping up something for a gift to the bride. Unfair I call it, the poor always having to give to the rich. Poor old Geta struggled to save this farthing by farthing from his rations, denying himself his pleasures, and now she'll make off with the lot, never stopping to think of the labour it cost him. Then he'll be stung for another present when she has a child, and after that there'll be birthdays and initiation ceremonies, all needing presents, and the mother takes all – the child is only an excuse for a present. But here *is* Geta.

[GETA, *a respectable middle-aged servant, comes out of his master* DEMIPHO's *house talking to someone inside.*]

GETA: If a red-head comes asking for me –

DAVOS: All right, he's here.

GETA: Oh Davos, I was just going to look for you.

DAVOS [*handing him the money*]: There you are, take it. It's all good money and the right amount.

GETA: Thanks for remembering it. I'm most grateful.

DAVOS: So you should be, the way things are today. We've come to the point of being 'most grateful' if a man does no more than pay his debts. But you look gloomy. What's the matter?

GETA: Do I? You don't know our fears and the danger we're in!

DAVOS: What do you mean?

GETA: I'll tell you; but don't breathe a word about it.

DAVOS: Go along, you idiot. If you can see a man's honest over money can't you trust him with a secret? And what'd I gain by deceiving you?

GETA: Then listen.

DAVOS: I am listening.

GETA: You know Chremes, our old man's elder brother?

DAVOS: Of course I do.

GETA: And his son Phaedria?

DAVOS: As well as I know you.

GETA: Well, it happened that both the old men went abroad at the same time, Chremes to Lemnos and Demipho to an old friend in Cilicia who had lured him over by promising him pretty well mountains of gold.

DAVOS: And him with wealth enough and to spare?

GETA: Oh well, that's his nature.

DAVOS: I wish I'd been born in a palace!

GETA: When they set off they both left me here as guardian to their sons.

DAVOS: That was a tough job.

GETA: So I found by experience. Looking back on it, my luck was out from the day they left. I began by trying to stand up to the boys – well, all I need say is that loyalty to my master's wishes just about broke my back.

DAVOS: Just as I thought: 'It's folly to kick against the pricks.'

GETA: Then I took to doing anything to please them and fell in with all their wishes.

DAVOS: You know how to work the market!

GETA: Young Antipho gave no trouble at first, but Phaedria promptly picked up a girl, some sort of a musician, and fell

head over ears in love with her. She was working for that
dirty pimp [*pointing to* DORIO's *house*] and there wasn't a
penny to pay for her; both fathers had seen to that. All he
could do was feast his eyes on her, follow her around, take
her to her music school and bring her back; I'd nothing to
do so I gave him all my attention. Right opposite her
school was a barber's shop where we generally waited for
her to come out and go home. We were sitting there one
day when a young man came in in tears. We were surprised,
and asked him what was the matter. 'Never before,' said he,
'did I realize the sheer misery and burden of poverty.
Round the corner I've just seen a pathetic young girl weeping for her dead mother. The body was laid out facing the
door, but there wasn't a single person, friend, acquaintance
or neighbour, except one old woman to help with the
funeral. It upset me terribly; and the girl's a beauty.' To cut
a long story short, we were all much touched by his story,
and suddenly Antipho cried, 'I say, shall we go and see her?'
Someone else said, 'Yes, let's, please take us.' We set out,
arrived, and saw her. She really was a lovely girl, and deserved to be called one all the more for being beauty unadorned – hair loose, bare feet, weeping and generally
dishevelled and dressed in mourning, all enough to hide her
looks if she hadn't had the gift of proper natural beauty.
Phaedria was taken up with his own girl, so all he said was
'Not bad.' But our Antipho –

DAVOS: I can guess; he fell for her.

GETA: Didn't he! Now mark what follows. Next day he goes
straight to the old woman and begs her to introduce him.
She refuses, says it wouldn't be right; the girl is an Attic
citizen, honest daughter of honest parents. If he wants her
for a wife he can marry her, all proper and legal. If it's

anything else, no. Antipho couldn't think what to do. He was dying to marry her and terrified of his absent father.

DAVOS: Wouldn't his father have given permission on his return?

GETA: What, him? Permission for his son to marry a girl with no dowry and no family? Never!

DAVOS: So what happened in the end?

GETA: You may well ask. There's a fellow called Phormio, one of those adventurers – devil take him for an impudent rascal.

DAVOS: How does he come in?

GETA: He gave us this advice. 'The law says that female orphans must be married to their next-of-kin, and the same law puts the next-of-kin under obligation to marry them. I'll say you are her relative and I'll take out a summons against you. I'll pretend to be a friend of the girl's father. We'll go to court; who her father was and her mother, and how she's related to you I can easily make up in the way that suits me best. You won't contest anything, so I'm sure to win. Of course your father will come back and I'll be in trouble, but no matter. We shall have got the girl.'

DAVOS: What cheek!

GETA: Antipho agreed, and everything else followed: summons, case, defeat, marriage.

DAVOS: You don't say so!

GETA: Well, you heard me.

DAVOS: But what'll become of *you*, Geta?

GETA: I've no idea [*striking a heroic attitude*]. All I know is that I shall meet my fate with dignity, come what may.

DAVOS: Splendid! There's heroism!

GETA: I can trust myself, none other.

DAVOS: Bravo!

GETA [*in his normal manner*]: And now I suppose I'd better find someone to plead my case: 'Let him off just this once, please, but if he's in trouble again he'll get no help from me.' Which amounts to saying 'As soon as I've gone you can hang him.'

DAVOS: What about the other fellow – the one who's got his eye on the musician? How's he getting on?

GETA: Phaedria? Not too well.

DAVOS: He hasn't much he can give, maybe?

GETA: Nothing at all but pure hope.

DAVOS: Is his father back yet or not?

GETA: Not yet.

DAVOS: And your old man, when do you expect him?

GETA: I don't really know, but I heard that a letter has just come from him and been handed in at the customs office. I'm going along to collect it now.

DAVOS: Nothing I can do, is there?

GETA: No, no, look after yourself. [DAVOS *goes off right and* GETA *knocks at* DEMIPHO's *door.*] Here, boy! Is there no one there? [*A slave boy comes out and* GETA *gives him the money-bag.*] Take this and give it to my wife.

  [*The boy goes in and* GETA *goes off left, to the harbour.* DEMIPHO's *door opens again and out come* ANTIPHO *and his cousin* PHAEDRIA, *both young men looking very gloomy and* ANTIPHO *in a great state of nerves.*]

ANTIPHO: Oh Phaedria, fancy things coming to this pass – I'm in terror of my father's return whenever I think of it! And yet he always had my best interests at heart, and if only I hadn't been so thoughtless I should have been expecting him in the right spirit.

PHAEDRIA [*wearily*]: What's the matter now?

ANTIPHO: You ought to know, as you had a hand in that

mad venture. I wish Phormio'd never thought of suggesting it. I wish I'd never been so eager to be pushed into it and landed myself with all this trouble. I shouldn't have had *her* and it would have been hell, but only for a few days, not this daily worry which is getting me down –

PHAEDRIA: Quite so.

ANTIPHO: – while all the time I'm waiting for him to come and take her away from me.

PHAEDRIA: Other people suffer through being *denied* what they love, but here you are groaning away over having too much of it. Yes, Antipho, you've got love and to spare – anyone would beg and pray for a life like yours. Good God, if I could enjoy my love as long, I'd be glad to die for it! Just you tot up all I get out of my nothing and you from your plenty, not counting the fact that without spending a penny you've got a girl who is free and well-born *and* have married her openly and honourably, just as you wanted. You've got everything to make you happy except the sense to know it. If you had to deal with that pimp as I do, you'd see! Most of us are like that I suppose, each one sorry for himself.

ANTIPHO: But you're the one I'd call fortunate, Phaedria. You're still quite free to decide what you really want, to keep her, love her or give her up. I'm in the unhappy position of knowing that the decision to keep her or not is out of my hands. [*He looks down the street, left.*] Now what – isn't that Geta I see running this way? Yes it is. Dear, dear, I'm sadly afraid he's bringing me bad news.

[*They move back as* GETA *hurries on, talking to himself.*]

GETA: You're done for, Geta, unless you can think of something at once – there's a storm of trouble threatening to break on you all unprepared for it. How to avoid or escape it I just don't know; that crazy business of ours can't be kept secret much longer.

ANTIPHO: What's put him in such a state?

GETA: Besides, I've only a minute . . . master's here.

ANTIPHO: What's his trouble?

GETA: Once he's heard something, he'll be furious and what shall I do? Tell him? It'll only infuriate him. Keep quiet? It'll make things worse. Defend myself? Labour wasted. Oh misery! I'm not only afraid for myself, I'm worried to death for Antipho – he's the trouble and worry, he's what's keeping me here. But for him I'd have looked after myself and got my own back on the old man for his temper: I'd have packed up and done a bolt.

ANTIPHO: Packing up? Bolting? What's the man thinking of?

GETA: Where *is* Antipho? [*Peering along the street*] Where am I to start looking for him?

PHAEDRIA [*pushing* ANTIPHO *forward*]: It's you he wants.

ANTIPHO [*shrinking back*]: I'm sure he's got something awful to tell me.

PHAEDRIA: Don't be a fool.

GETA: I'll go home, he's usually there.

PHAEDRIA: Let's call him back.

ANTIPHO: Stop!

GETA [*scarcely turning his head*]: What? Pretty free with your orders aren't you, whoever you are.

ANTIPHO: Geta!

GETA [*coming back*]: Why it's you, sir, the very man I wanted.

ANTIPHO: Now then please, give me your news and be quick about it.

GETA: All right.

ANTIPHO: Then tell me.

GETA: Just now at the harbour –

ANTIPHO: You saw my –

GETA: You've got it.

ANTIPHO: There, I'm finished.

PHAEDRIA: I say –

ANTIPHO: What shall I do?

PHAEDRIA: What's all this?

GETA [*to* PHAEDRIA]: I saw his father, your uncle.

ANTIPHO [*pacing about distractedly*]: Oh, what a disastrous situation! How can I get out of it? If it's my fate to be torn from you, Phanium, no life's worth living.

GETA: Come, come, sir, as things are there's all the more reason for making an effort. Fortune favours the brave.

ANTIPHO: I can't pull myself together.

GETA: But this is the moment when you *must*, sir. If your father sees you looking nervous he'll guess you've done something wrong.

PHAEDRIA: Geta's quite right.

ANTIPHO: No good, I can't change.

GETA: What if you had something even harder to face?

ANTIPHO: If I can't cope with this I'd be even less able with that.

GETA: Oh he's hopeless, sir, leave him. Why waste more time on him? I'm going.

PHAEDRIA: So am I.

[*They start to move off when* ANTIPHO *catches at them.*]

ANTIPHO: No, please; what if I pretended – would that do?

GETA: Don't be silly.

ANTIPHO [*trying to look resolute*]: Look at my face, both of you. Is that all right?

GETA: No.

ANTIPHO: What about this?

GETA: Nearly.

ANTIPHO: Like this then?

GETA: That'll do. Now keep it up. Answer him word for word, hit for hit, or he'll bowl you over in his savage bursts of fury.

ANTIPHO: I know.

GETA: Say you were forced into it against your will.

PHAEDRIA: By the law, by order of court.

GETA: Understand? Now I can see an old man at the end of the street. . . . Yes, it's the master all right.

ANTIPHO [*his resolution rapidly leaving him*]: I can't stay –

GETA: Hi, what are you doing? Where are you going? Stop, sir, can't you –

ANTIPHO: I know myself and what I've done. I'm leaving Phanium and my life in your hands.

　　[*He disappears along the street right.*]

PHAEDRIA: What'll happen now, Geta?

GETA: You're in for a row, sir, and I'll be strung up and flogged unless I'm much mistaken. But our duty now is to follow the advice we gave Antipho.

PHAEDRIA: Never mind about duty, just tell me what to do.

GETA: Do you remember the excuse you both originally decided to make to your uncle: that Phormio had right and justice on his side and you hadn't a hope of defeating him?

PHAEDRIA: I remember.

GETA: We'll have to use that now if we can't think of something better and cleverer.

PHAEDRIA: I'll do my best.

GETA [*who is watching* DEMIPHO's *approach off-stage*]: Now you go in to attack while I lie in ambush as a reserve in case you have to give ground.

PHAEDRIA: Come on then.

[*They both stand back as* DEMIPHO *comes on left, tired after his journey and exasperated by the news which has already reached his ears.*]

DEMIPHO [*to himself*]: So that's it – my son has married without my permission! With no regard for my outraged feelings – let alone my authority – no sense of shame! A disgraceful piece of impudence! So much for Geta as a guardian!

GETA [*to* PHAEDRIA]: I wondered when he was coming to me.

DEMIPHO: What will they say to me – what excuse will they find? I wonder.

GETA: I'll find one, don't worry.

DEMIPHO: Perhaps he'll say, 'I didn't want to do it: the law compelled me.' Precisely, I grant that.

GETA: Good.

DEMIPHO: But did the law also compel him to throw up the case to the prosecution, without a word?

PHAEDRIA: That's quite a problem.

GETA: Leave it to me, I'll solve it.

DEMIPHO: Now what am I to do? The whole thing is so unforeseen and unexpected, and I'm so angry I can't think straight. It just shows that when things look best it's the time for us all to be thinking how to bear the worst – dangers, losses and exile – and a man returning from abroad should always have in mind the common misfortunes which may be waiting for him, a son's misdeeds, death of a wife and sickness of a daughter; so that nothing takes him by surprise, and anything which betters his expectations can be counted pure gain.

GETA [*to* PHAEDRIA]: I could never have believed that I was wiser than my master, sir, but I've been thinking of all the misfortunes awaiting *me* when he returned, flogging, fetters, grinding at the mill and toiling at the farm. .... None of this will take me by surprise, and anything which betters my expectations I'll count pure gain. But why don't you approach him, sir? Say something soothing for a start.

[PHAEDRIA *comes forward and greets* DEMIPHO *effusively.*]

PHAEDRIA: Good morning, Uncle.

DEMIPHO [*curtly*]: Good morning. Where is Antipho?

PHAEDRIA: I'm delighted to see you –

DEMIPHO: I don't doubt it. Answer my question.

PHAEDRIA: He's very well, he's somewhere around. .... Is everything all right with you?

DEMIPHO: I only wish it were!

PHAEDRIA: What do you mean, Uncle?

DEMIPHO: Don't ask silly questions. A fine marriage you people have arranged for him while I was away.

PHAEDRIA [*with a great show of astonishment*]: Is *that* why you're angry with him?

GETA [*aside*]: Oh, good show!

DEMIPHO: Is there any reason why I should *not* be angry? All I want is to have him here before me so that he can see how his conduct has changed his indulgent father into one of very different temper.

PHAEDRIA: But Uncle, he hasn't done anything to make you angry.

DEMIPHO: There you are! All of a pattern, all the same. Know one, you know the lot.

PHAEDRIA: That's not true.

DEMIPHO: A's at fault, B's on the spot to defend him. Reverse them, and A's there to defend B. It's a mutual benefit society.

GETA [*aside*]: The old man's drawn them to the life if he did but know it.

DEMIPHO: If it weren't so, Phaedria, you wouldn't be taking his side.

PHAEDRIA [*virtuously*]: If Antipho has really done wrong, Uncle, and been careless of his property and reputation, I'm not arguing against his getting what he deserves. But if some ill-natured person has successfully laid a trap for inexperienced youth, is that our fault? Shouldn't you blame the courts which often take from the rich in spite and give to the poor out of pity?

GETA [*aside*]: If I didn't know the facts I'd think he spoke the truth.

DEMIPHO: How can a court give the right decision if the defendant is as dumb as Antipho was?

PHAEDRIA: What do you expect from a well-brought-up young man? Once in court he couldn't find words for his carefully prepared defence. He's naturally shy, and on this occasion was struck dumb with nervousness.

GETA [*aside*]: He's doing well. This is where I come in. [*Coming forward*] Good morning, sir. I'm glad to see you safely back again.

DEMIPHO: Good morning, faithful guardian, prop and mainstay of my home, to whom I entrusted my son when I went abroad!

GETA: I've been listening for some time, sir, to your unjust charges against us all – including me who deserves them least of anybody. What did you want me to do for you in all this? The law doesn't permit a slave to plead in court or give evidence.

DEMIPHO: I know, I know. The boy's nervous and inexperienced and you're a slave. But however closely the girl is supposed to be related to us, there was no need for him to *marry* her. You could have supplied the dowry the law demands and she could have looked for another husband; instead of which he goes and brings home a penniless wife. What's the sense of it?

GETA: It wasn't sense we lacked, it was cash.

DEMIPHO: He could have borrowed it from somewhere.

GETA: Somewhere? Easily said.

DEMIPHO: On interest, if all else failed.

GETA: That's the best I've heard! Who'd give him credit while you're alive?

DEMIPHO: I won't have it, I tell you! It's impossible. I refuse to allow this marriage for another day. They deserve no consideration. Now kindly point out that individual, or show me where he lives.

GETA: You mean Phormio?

DEMIPHO: I mean the man who acted for the girl.

GETA: I'll have him here in no time.

DEMIPHO: And now where's Antipho?

GETA: Gone out.

DEMIPHO: Phaedria, you go find him and bring him here.

PHAEDRIA: All right Uncle, I'll go straight – there [*with a wink at* GETA *and gesture at* DORIO'S *house where* PAMPHILA *is; he then pretends to go off right but slips in unnoticed*].

GETA [*aside*]: I know, to Pamphila.
　　　[*He goes off, right.*]

DEMIPHO: I'm going in to give thanks to the gods for my return. Then I shall go into town to find some friends to support me. I must be ready for Phormio when he comes.
　　　[*He goes into his house. After a short interval, a smart and self-confident young man comes on jauntily from the right; here at last is* PHORMIO. *With him is* GETA.]

PHORMIO: You say he went off in a panic when his father arrived?

GETA: Yes.

PHORMIO: Then Phanium's alone?

GETA: Yes.

PHORMIO: And the old man is furious?

GETA: He certainly is.

PHORMIO: Then it all devolves on you, Phormio. It's your cooking, you must eat it. Prepare for action!

GETA: Please –

PHORMIO [*ignoring him*]: Now if he asks –

GETA: You're our only hope –

PHORMIO [*still to himself*]: Look, suppose he replies . . .

GETA: It was you who pushed us into this –

PHORMIO: . . . That'll do, I think.

GETA: Please help us.

PHORMIO [*condescending to listen at last*]: Bring on the old man. My plans are laid.

GETA: What'll you do?

PHORMIO: What do you want? Antipho rescued from this charge, Phanium to remain his wife and the full flood of the old man's wrath to be diverted on to me?

GETA: You're a brave man, Phormio, and a good friend. All the same I often have my fears that this sort of bravery will end by landing you in jail.

PHORMIO: Nothing of the sort. I've tested the path and know where to put my feet. I've had men beaten up, foreigners and citizens, nearly to death: do you know how many? The better I know my way, the more I've dealt with. Well, have you ever heard of my being charged with assault?

GETA: No. How do you manage it?

PHORMIO: The net isn't spread for harmful birds like the hawk or kite but for the harmless ones which are profitable to catch. The others are waste labour. There are all sorts of

risks for people who can be fleeced, but everyone knows
I've got nothing. You may say they'll get me convicted
and hauled off to slave for them, but who wants to feed an
appetite like mine? So if they don't choose to give a villain
a due reward, I'd say they're only showing sense.

GETA: My young master will never be able to repay you
properly.

PHORMIO: Ah no, it's a man's patron who can never be repaid.
You contribute nothing, but come to dinner washed and
scented after a bath without a care in the world while *he* is
harassed by worry and expense. Everything's done for your
pleasure while he can only make faces; you're the one
who smiles, takes first seat and first drink. Then a – difficult
sort of dinner is set before you.

GETA: What do you mean, difficult?

PHORMIO: Difficult to decide what you'll take first. And when
you start reckoning how delicious and costly it all is, won't
you look upon its provider as your patron god?

GETA [*looking down the street*]: Here's old Demipho. Now look
out – first blows count most. If you can hold your ground
now you can play with him afterwards as you please.

[DEMIPHO *comes on right* with his three legal advisers; the
others stand back.*]

DEMIPHO: Did you ever hear of such an outrageous insult?
Stand by me, please.

GETA [*to* PHORMIO]: He's in a temper.

PHORMIO: Now play up; I'm going to tease him. [*Aloud, so
that* DEMIPHO *can hear their pretended quarrel*] Good God,

---

*As Demipho went into his house at l. 314, he must have gone out
by the back door. (In the Greek play an altar stood on the stage, so he
could have offered his thanks to the gods without going in. See *The
Girl from Andros*, p. 57.)

does Demipho really deny the relationship? Does he actuall
say that Phanium is *not* related to him?

GETA: Yes, he does.

PHORMIO: And says he doesn't know who her father was?

GETA: That's right.

DEMIPHO [*to his friends*]: I believe that's the man. Follow me

PHORMIO: Says he never knew Stilpo?

GETA: That's right.

PHORMIO: Just because that poor girl is left penniless, he
father's disowned and she is cast off. See what avarice does

GETA [*in mock defence*]: If you're out to charge my master with
bad faith you'll only get yourself a bad name.

DEMIPHO: What impudence! I do believe he's going to turn
the charge against me.

PHORMIO: Mind you, I've nothing against young Antipho i
he didn't know Stilpo, for he was getting on in years and
pretty hard up, worked for his living and spent nearly al
his time in the country where he had a bit of land from my
father. He often used to tell me how this relative of hi
ignored his existence; but what a man he was! One of th
best I ever set eyes on.

GETA: Then you could see about being more like him – i
we're to believe your tale.

PHORMIO: Oh go to hell! If I hadn't thought well of him
should I be quarrelling with your household on behalf o
his daughter – who is rejected by your master in this shabby
fashion?

GETA: Will you kindly stop abusing him behind his back, you
foul-mouthed brute?

PHORMIO: Abuse is just about what he deserves.

GETA [*threateningly*]: What's that you're saying, jail-bird?

DEMIPHO: Geta!

GETA: Robber! Perjurer!

DEMIPHO: Geta!

PHORMIO [*aside*]: Answer him.

GETA [*coming forward*]: Who's that? Oh it's you, sir.

DEMIPHO: Be quiet.

GETA: He's been carrying on behind your back all day, sir, with insults better suited to himself.

DEMIPHO: Be quiet. [*To* PHORMIO, *who comes forward*] By your leave, young man, perhaps you'll be so good as to answer me one question: who exactly was this man you say was your friend, and how did he say I was related to him?

PHORMIO [*insolently*]: Fishing for information, are you, as if you didn't know him?

DEMIPHO: *I* knew him?

PHORMIO: You knew him all right.

DEMIPHO: I deny it. But as you say I did, please refresh my memory.

PHORMIO: Why, don't you know your own cousin?

DEMIPHO: Stop this tomfoolery and tell me his name.

PHORMIO: His name? Certainly.

[*There is a pause.*]

DEMIPHO: Then why don't you say it?

PHORMIO: Dear me, I've forgotten it.

DEMIPHO: What's that?

PHORMIO [*aside*]: Geta, can you remember the name I used before? Whisper it. [*To* DEMIPHO] I'm not saying it. You're up to some trick, pretending you don't know him.

DEMIPHO: What do you mean, up to some trick?

GETA [*in* PHORMIO'*s ear*]: Stilpo.

PHORMIO: Oh I might as well tell you. It's Stilpo.

DEMIPHO: What did you say?

PHORMIO [*with exaggerated clarity*]: The – man – you – knew
   was – Stilpo.

DEMIPHO: Never heard of him. No one of that name ha
   ever been related to me.

PHORMIO: Really? You ought to be ashamed of yoursel
   before these gentlemen here. Of course if he'd left you a fev
   thousands –

DEMIPHO: Damn you!

PHORMIO: – you'd be the first to trace your family tree i
   detail right back to your grandfather and great-grandfathe

DEMIPHO [*trying hard to keep his temper*]: Quite so. And if
   had been present I should have said how the girl was sup
   posed to be related to me. You do so now: come on, how
   she my relative?

GETA: Well done, our side! [*To* PHORMIO] Now, look ou

PHORMIO: I made a clear statement in the proper place, i
   court. If it wasn't correct, why didn't your son refute it?

DEMIPHO: Don't talk to me of my son. When it comes to h
   stupidity, words fail me.

PHORMIO: Well, you're no fool. You go to the magistrat
   and ask for a new trial. You're top dog here and the onl
   person likely to get the same case heard twice.

DEMIPHO: This is sheer victimization, but sooner than hav
   to go to law – and listen to you – I'll assume she *is* my rela
   tive and give her the dowry the law prescribes. Here's fiv
   hundred drachmas, now get her out of my house.

PHORMIO [*laughing scornfully and waving the proffered mone
   away*]: Very nice, I'm sure.

DEMIPHO: *Now* what? Isn't that a fair proposal? Am I to b
   denied common justice?

PHORMIO: Do you really mean to tell me that this law exis
   to enable a man to pay off a kept woman and get rid of he

when he's had his pleasure? Or was it to prevent any
Athenian woman's having to disgrace herself through
poverty that she was ordered by law to marry her nearest
relative and live with him alone? This is what you are trying
to prevent.

DEMIPHO: Yes, her nearest relative. But where do *we* come
in? And why?

PHORMIO: Now, now; 'what's done can't be undone'.

DEMIPHO: Can't be undone? On the contrary, I shan't rest
until I see that it is.

PHORMIO: Nonsense.

DEMIPHO: You wait and see.

PHORMIO: One last word, Demipho; we're not interested in
you. The court dealt with your son, not you. [*Rudely*] You're
past the age of marrying.

DEMIPHO: You can take it that all I'm saying to you comes
from him too. Otherwise I shall forbid him the house along
with that wife of his.

GETA [*aside to* PHORMIO]: He's furious.

PHORMIO: You'd do better to keep out yourself.

DEMIPHO: Then you are prepared to oppose anything I do,
you poor fool?

PHORMIO [*to* GETA]: He's afraid of us, however much he tries
to hide it.

GETA [*to* PHORMIO]: You've made a jolly good start.

PHORMIO: Why can't you bow to the inevitable? Do what's
best and let us be friends.

DEMIPHO: Do you expect *me* to seek *your* friendship? I never
want to see or hear you again.

PHORMIO: If you could reconcile yourself to *her* you'd have
someone to amuse you in your old age. You're not getting
any younger you know.

DEMIPHO: You keep her then. *You* can be amused.

PHORMIO: Temper, temper!

DEMIPHO: Listen to me; we've said quite enough. If you don't hurry up and remove that woman from my house I shall throw her out. That's my last word, Phormio.

PHORMIO: She's a free citizen, and if you so much as lay a finger on her I'll bring an action which will finish you. And that's *my* last word, Demipho. [*Beckoning to* GETA] If I'm wanted, I'm at home.

GETA: I see.

[PHORMIO *swaggers off right, pleased with himself.*]

DEMIPHO [*to himself*]: Oh the trouble and worry that boy has given me by entangling us both in this marriage! And he doesn't even show his face so that at least I could know what he has to say for himself and what he thinks about it all. Geta, go and see if he has come home yet or not.

GETA: Very good, sir.

[*He goes into* DEMIPHO's *house and* DEMIPHO *turns to his three friends who have been listening and perhaps taking a few notes.*]

DEMIPHO: You see the situation. What shall I do? You tell me, Hegio.

HEGIO: Me? I think Cratinus would be better, if you don't mind.

DEMIPHO: Then you, Cratinus.

CRATINUS: Me?

DEMIPHO: Yes, you.

CRATINUS [*after a lot of thought*]: I should like you to act in your best interests. In my view your son's actions during your absence should rightly and properly be rendered null and void: and you will succeed in this. That is my opinion.

DEMIPHO: Now Hegio.

HEGIO: I am sure Cratinus has delivered a carefully considered opinion. But the truth is, there are as many opinions as there are men to give them, no two think alike. I cannot agree that a legally pronounced judgement can be quashed; and it would be discreditable to attempt it.

DEMIPHO: Now you, Crito.

CRITO [*after a long pause*]: I must have time to consider my opinion. It is a difficult case.

[*There is another long and embarrassing silence, broken by* CRATINUS *asking politely*:]

CRATINUS: Have you further need of us?

DEMIPHO: No, no, you have done very well. [*They go off right with dignity.*] I'm more muddled than ever.

[GETA *comes out of the house.*]

GETA: They say he's not back, sir.

DEMIPHO: I shall have to wait for my brother. He'll have some advice for me to follow. I'll go along to the harbour and find out when he's due.

[*He goes off, left.*]

GETA: And I'll find Antipho and tell him what's been happening here. [*He sets off right and then stops.*] Good, here he is on his way back.

[ANTIPHO *comes on right, preoccupied with his troubles.*]

ANTIPHO: In fact, Antipho, you've mostly yourself and your lack of spirit to blame – dashing off like that and leaving your life in other folks' hands. Did you suppose they would look after your interests better than you could yourself? And quite apart from that, you should have given a thought to that poor girl who is in your house at the present moment and not left her to suffer through her misplaced trust in you. You're her only hope now, she depends on you for everything.

GETA [*coming forward*]: Just what we've been saying, sir, all the time you were away. You ought never to have gone off like that.

ANTIPHO: Geta! I was looking for you.

GETA: Were you, sir? Anyway, we didn't wait to do what we can for you.

ANTIPHO: Please tell me, how are things going? Any luck? Has my father suspected anything?

GETA: Well . . . not yet.

ANTIPHO: Is there any hope then?

GETA: I can't really say.

ANTIPHO [*groans*]

GETA: But Phaedria's never stopped trying everything.

ANTIPHO: He always does.

GETA: And Phormio's been playing an active part, as usual.

ANTIPHO: What's he been doing?

GETA: Talking to the old man when he got worked up and calming him down.

ANTIPHO: Good old Phormio!

GETA [*modestly*]: I've done all I can too, sir.

ANTIPHO [*hugging him*]: Geta, dear man, thank you all.

GETA: The first round's over, as I say, and things are still quiet. Your father's waiting until your uncle arrives.

ANTIPHO: What does he want out of him?

GETA: He says he wants to follow his advice, at any rate in this matter.

ANTIPHO [*dashed again*]: Oh dear, Geta, how I dread my uncle's safe arrival! I know he's only got to say the word and I'm dead – or alive!

GETA: Here comes Phaedria, sir.

ANTIPHO: Where?

GETA: Coming away from his private wrestling-ground.

[PHAEDRIA *and the pimp* DORIO *come out of* DORIO's *house, arguing.*]

PHAEDRIA: Dorio, do listen, please –

DORIO: I won't.

PHAEDRIA: Just a word –

DORIO: No. Leave me alone.

PHAEDRIA: Do listen to what I'm saying.

DORIO: I'm sick of listening to you. It's the same thing all the time.

PHAEDRIA: But this time I'll say something you *want* to hear.

DORIO: All right, I'm listening.

PHAEDRIA: Can't I persuade you to wait – just for the next three days? [DORIO *makes a move towards his house.*] Now where are you going?

DORIO: I thought it was queer if you'd something new to tell me.

ANTIPHO: Geta, I'm afraid this man is –

GETA [*drily*]: Asking for trouble? Oh yes, I'm afraid of that too.

PHAEDRIA: Don't you trust me?

DORIO: However did you guess that?

PHAEDRIA: If I give you my word?

DORIO: Nonsense.

PHAEDRIA: You'll say your kindness was a good investment.

DORIO: Rubbish!

PHAEDRIA: Believe me, you'll be glad you did it. That's true, honest it is.

DORIO: Moonshine.

PHAEDRIA: Just *try*; it isn't for long.

DORIO: The same old story.

PHAEDRIA: I count you one of the family, a father, a real friend, a –

DORIO: Talk on, talk on.

PHAEDRIA: How can you be so stubborn and hard-hearted?
You won't be softened by pity or prayers.

DORIO: How can *you* be so impudent and dim-witted? You
think you can move me by fancy words and make off with
a girl of mine for nothing.

ANTIPHO [*to* GETA]: That's his way of showing pity.

PHAEDRIA [*tearfully*]: True, I suppose; he's got me there.

GETA: How the pair of them run true to type!

PHAEDRIA: And the blow didn't fall when Antipho was
having *his* bit of trouble. . . .

ANTIPHO [*coming forward*]: Whatever is the matter, Phaedria?

PHAEDRIA: Oh Antipho, you lucky, lucky man –

ANTIPHO: *Me* lucky?

PHAEDRIA: Yes. You've got the one you love at home. You've
never known what it is to be battling against this sort of
misfortune.

ANTIPHO: Got her at home? I'd say I've the proverbial wolf
by the ears – can't let go and can't hold on.

DORIO: That exactly how I am with him.

ANTIPHO [*to* DORIO]: Come, come, you should know your
job. [*To* PHAEDRIA, *indicating* DORIO] Has he been up to
anything?

PHAEDRIA: What do you think? This beastly brute has sold
my Pamphila.

ANTIPHO: Sold her?

GETA: Did you say he'd *sold* her?

PHAEDRIA: Sold her.

DORIO: Can't a man sell a girl he bought and paid for?
What's wrong in that?

PHAEDRIA: I can't persuade him to cancel his offer with the
other fellow and wait – just for the next three days until

can raise the money promised by my friends. [*To* DORIO]
If I don't pay you then, you needn't wait another hour.

DORIO: Carry on, don't mind me.

ANTIPHO: He isn't asking for long, Dorio. Come on, say yes.
Do him this service and he'll repay it twice over.

DORIO: So you say.

ANTIPHO: Are you going to let Pamphila be sent away from
Athens? Can you see these two lovers torn apart like this?

DORIO: Well, we can't stop it, can we?

PHAEDRIA: Then I hope the gods will see you get your deserts!

DORIO: Look here, I've put up with you against my better
judgement for a good many months, with your promises
and tears and never a penny paid up. Now I've found the
exact opposite: someone who'll pay – and no tears. You
stand down for your betters.

ANTIPHO: Surely, if I remember rightly, there was a day
fixed for you to pay him?

PHAEDRIA: Yes, there was.

DORIO: Am I denying it?

ANTIPHO: Is it past the date?

DORIO: No, but the new one's come first.

ANTIPHO: That's double-crossing. Aren't you ashamed?

DORIO: Not in the least, so long as I'm making something out
of it.

GETA: You – you muck-heap!

ANTIPHO: Dorio, seriously, ought you to behave like this?

DORIO [*with a shrug*]: It's how I am. If you like me, you'll find
I have my uses.

ANTIPHO: Cheating Phaedria like this!

DORIO: Actually it's he who's cheating *me*, Antipho. He
knew all along what I was like, but I thought he was quite
different. He's deceived me, but I've been the same as I've

always been. However, let it pass. This is what I'll do: the
Captain promised to pay me the money tomorrow morning. If you can bring it before then, Phaedria, I'll stick to my
rule of first pay first served. Good-bye.

[*He bows and goes into his house, slamming the door.*]

PHAEDRIA: Now what shall I do? Just my luck! Wherever
can I find him the money so soon? I'm completely broke. If
only I'd been able to get the three days out of him, I had it
promised.

ANTIPHO: Geta, we can't leave him in his misery like this,
when he was so good about helping me, so you told
me. We simply must try to repay his kindness now he
needs us.

GETA [*dubiously*]: I know that's the right thing to do.

ANTIPHO: Well, come on then, you're the only one who can
save him.

GETA: What can *I* do?

ANTIPHO: Find the money.

GETA: Nothing I'd like better: but just you show me where.

ANTIPHO: My father's home again.

GETA: I know, but how does that help?

ANTIPHO: A word's enough for the wise . . .

GETA: You don't mean –

ANTIPHO: Yes, I do.

GETA: Very nice, sir, I'm sure. Oh get away with you! Isn't it
triumph enough for me to have escaped trouble over your
own wedding without being told to stick my neck out for
your cousin here?

ANTIPHO [*to* PHAEDRIA]: He's right, you know.

PHAEDRIA: What? Don't you count me one of the family,
Geta?

GETA: I suppose I do. But the old man's mad enough with the

lot of us as it is without us goading him on until we'll never be able to beg for mercy.

PHAEDRIA [*dramatically*]: Shall another man snatch her off to an unknown land before my very eyes? Ah, speak to me, Antipho, look on me here and now while you can, while you have me still with you –

ANTIPHO: What for? What are you going to do? Come on, tell us.

PHAEDRIA: Whatever part of the world shall be her destination I am determined to follow her – or die.

GETA: Heaven help your plans, sir, but not too quickly.

ANTIPHO [*to* GETA]: See if you can give him any help.

GETA: Any help? What help?

ANTIPHO: Do please *think* or he may do something we'll be sorry for later on.

GETA: I'm thinking . . . [*After a pause evidently an idea comes to him.*] He'll be all right, I do believe – but I'm afraid there'll be trouble.

ANTIPHO: Don't be afraid. We're all in this together, whatever happens.

GETA [*to* PHAEDRIA]: First tell me how much money you need.

PHAEDRIA: Only three thousand drachmas.

GETA: Three thousand? She's very expensive, sir.

PHAEDRIA [*indignantly*]: At that price she's cheap.

GETA: All right, all right, I'll see you have it.

PHAEDRIA [*hugging him*]: Geta, you're a darling!

GETA [*primly disengaging himself*]: That will do, sir.

PHAEDRIA: I must have it at once.

GETA: You *shall* have it at once; but I must have Phormio to help me.

PHAEDRIA: He'll be with you. Put any burden on him you

like and he'll shoulder it manfully. He's the best friend you could have.

GETA: Hurry up then and find him.

ANTIPHO: Is there anything I can do for you?

GETA: Nothing. Go home and comfort your poor Phanium, who must be waiting there half-dead with fright. Hurry along now!

ANTIPHO: There's nothing I'd rather do.

[*He hurries into* DEMIPHO's *house.*]

PHAEDRIA: How on earth are you going to manage this?

GETA: I'll tell you on the way. Come on, sir.

[*They go off right in search of* PHORMIO *and so miss* DEMIPHO *and his brother* CHREMES *who come on left, from the harbour.*]

DEMIPHO: Now, Chremes, what about the purpose which took you to Lemnos? Have you brought back your daughter?

CHREMES: No.

DEMIPHO: Why not?

CHREMES: Because her mother had already left to look for me – so I was told. She thought I was never coming back from Athens, and the girl was growing up and couldn't wait while I neglected her, so she packed up everything and set out with all her household to join me.

DEMIPHO: Then why did you stay there so long when you heard this?

CHREMES: I was ill and couldn't get away.

DEMIPHO: What was the matter? Where did you catch it?

CHREMES: Never mind; it's illness enough to be old. But I heard they had arrived here safely from the sailor who brought them.

DEMIPHO: Have you heard what happened to my son while I
   was away?

CHREMES: Yes, I have, and it puts *me* in a quandary now about
   my daughter's marriage. If I try to make a match for her
   outside the family I shall have to give a proper account of
   how she comes to be my daughter. I knew my secret was as
   safe with you as with myself, but any outsider who wants to
   marry into my family will hold his tongue only so long as
   we are on good terms. If we fall out he'll soon know more
   than he need. I'm terrified too of my wife's getting to hear
   about this somehow – if that happens all I can do is to throw
   everything up and clear out; my person is the only thing in
   the house I can call my own.

DEMIPHO: I realize that, and the whole thing is a great worry
   to me. I shall go on trying everything I can in the hope
   of carrying out our previous arrangement.

   [*They move aside, still deep in conversation, and so do not see*
   GETA *hurrying on right.*]

GETA [*to himself*]: I've never seen a man so quick-witted as
   Phormio. I came to tell him we needed money and find out
   how we could get it. I'd scarcely spoken before he'd got the
   point. He was delighted, congratulated me and asked to see
   the master. He thanked heaven for giving him the chance to
   show himself as much the friend of Phaedria as of Antipho.
   I told him to wait for me in the market-place and I'd bring
   the old man along. ... But there he is – and who's
   that behind him? My God, it's Phaedria's father come home!
   Now you ass, no need to panic if you've got two to handle
   instead of one. It's better to have two targets for one's bow
   I suppose. I'll aim at the one I first had in mind. If he pays up
   that'll do. If there's nothing doing with him I'll tackle the
   new arrival.

[ANTIPHO *opens the door of* DEMIPHO'*s house and stands
listening.*]

ANTIPHO: I'll just wait for Geta – I wonder how soon he'll be
back. Oh damn, there's my uncle with my father. I dread
to think what effect his arrival will have.

GETA: Now for it. [*He approaches* CHREMES] Oh sir –

CHREMES [*curtly*]: Well, Geta.

GETA: I'm delighted to see you safely back, sir.

CHREMES: Doubtless.

GETA [*nervously*]: How are things with you, sir? One always
comes home to find a good many changes.

CHREMES: A *great* many changes.

GETA: Yes, sir. You've heard about your nephew Antipho?

CHREMES [*grimly*]: Yes. Everything.

GETA [*to* DEMIPHO]: Was it you who told him, sir? Shocking
isn't it, to find what's done behind your back like this.

CHREMES: I was discussing it with my brother just now.

GETA [*catching at his opportunity*]: And I've never stopped
thinking about it too, sir, but now I do believe I've found a
solution.

CHREMES: What is it?

DEMIPHO: What solution?

GETA: When I left you, sir, I ran into Phormio.

CHREMES: Who's Phormio?

GETA: The girl's –

CHREMES: I remember.

GETA: I thought I'd sound his opinion so I took him aside.
'Phormio,' I said, 'why don't you see that we settle this
matter between us in a friendly spirit with no ill feeling?
My master is generous and hates lawsuits, but the fact is that
all his friends without exception have been telling him with
one voice to throw the girl out of his house.'

ANTIPHO [*aside*]: What's he up to? What's his idea?

GETA: 'You may say he'll have the law after him if he turns her out, but that's all been worked out. *You*'ll be the one in trouble if you let yourself be involved with that man. You should hear his eloquence! Even supposing he loses, it isn't his life and liberty at stake, only his money.' I saw my words were beginning to have some effect on him, so I went on: 'We're alone here at the moment, so just you name the price you want for my master to drop his present suit, the girl to take herself off, and you to stop making a nuisance of yourself.'

ANTIPHO: Has he gone off his head?

GETA: 'He's an honest gentleman,' I said, 'and I'm quite sure if there's anything fair and honest in the terms you offer it can all be settled at once between you in a couple of words.'

DEMIPHO [*coldly*]: And who gave you authority to talk like this?

CHREMES: No, no, he's right. It's the best way of getting what we want.

ANTIPHO: That finishes me!

DEMIPHO: Continue.

GETA: At first the man was furious.

CHREMES [*impatiently*]: How much did he want?

GETA: Far too much. The first sum which came into his head.

CHREMES: *Tell* me.

GETA: He talked of six thousand –

DEMIPHO: And he'll get something much less pleasant. What impudence!

GETA: Just what I told him, sir. 'Good heavens,' I said. 'He might be marrying off his one and only daughter! He's not gained much by not bringing up a daughter of his own if someone else turns up demanding a dowry like that.' To cut a long story short and pass over his impertinence, this was his final proposal: 'I always wanted to do the right thing and marry my friend's daughter, and I kept thinking how she'd suffer for her poverty if she had to slave for a rich husband, but to be quite frank with you, I needed a wife who could bring me a bit to pay off my debts. Still, if Demipho is willing to give me as much as I'm getting from the girl who's now engaged to me, I'd rather have Phanium for a wife than anyone.'

ANTIPHO: Is this malice or sheer stupidity? Does the man know what he's doing or not? I've no idea.

DEMIPHO: What if he's up to the eyes in debt?

GETA: 'There's some land,' he said, 'mortgaged for a thousand.'

DEMIPHO: All right, all right, let him marry her at once. I'll pay that.

GETA: 'A small house too for another thousand.'

DEMIPHO: No. That's too much.

CHREMES: Don't fuss. You can have that thousand from me.

GETA: 'My wife must have a maid, and we shall need a few sticks of furniture; then there's the expense of the wedding. You can reckon all this as another thousand.'

DEMIPHO: Well then, he can bring six hundred actions against me: I'm not paying a penny. Does the scoundrel think he can fool me?

CHREMES: Calm yourself, please; I'll pay. All you need do is see that your son marries the girl we intended for him.

ANTIPHO: Damn you, Geta, your tricks have been the death of me.

CHREMES: She's being turned out on my account, so it's only right that I should stand the loss.

GETA: 'Let me know as soon as possible,' he said, 'so that I can get rid of my present girl if they'll let me have the other one. I don't want things left in the air, as the other family has agreed to pay me the dowry at once.'

CHREMES [*eagerly*]: He shall have it at once, break it off with them and marry her.

DEMIPHO: And much good may it do him!

CHREMES: Luckily I've got money with me now, the rent from my wife's property in Lemnos. I'll take it from that and tell her you needed it.

[*They go into* CHREMES' *house without seeing* ANTIPHO, *who now steps forward.*]

ANTIPHO: Geta!

GETA: Yes, sir?

ANTIPHO: What *have* you been doing?

GETA [*well pleased with himself*]: Diddling the old men out of their money, sir.

ANTIPHO: Was that all?

GETA: Damned if I know. It's all I was told to get.

ANTIPHO: You wretch, can't you answer my question?

GETA: What do you mean then?

ANTIPHO: I mean that the rope's round my neck and it's clear you put it there. May all the deities of heaven and hell condemn you to utter damnation! [*To the audience*] Look here, anything you want done just give it to *him* – if you want a proper job made of it. [*To* GETA] What good could it possibly do to touch on that sore spot and drag in my wife's name? You've buoyed my father up with hopes of getting her out of the house. And what's more: if Phormio takes the dowry she'll have to marry *him*. What'll happen then?

GETA: But he won't marry her.

ANTIPHO: Oh no, of course not. And when they want the

money back I suppose he'll choose to go to jail on our behalf.

GETA: Look here, sir, everything sounds worse if it's told all wrong. You leave out all the good bits and only mention the bad ones. Just you look at it this way; granted that if he takes the money he must marry her, as you say; but there must be a little time for the wedding preparations, sending out invitations and arranging the service. Meanwhile his friends will give him what they've promised and he'll pay it back out of that.

ANTIPHO: But why should he? What reason will he give?

GETA: Well, if you must know, he could say: 'I've had so many warnings since then – a strange black dog came into my house, a snake fell from the tiles through the skylight, a hen crowed, a soothsayer spoke against it and a diviner forbade it. Nothing now, please, until after the winter solstice.' That's the best kind of excuse; and that's the sort of thing he'll say.

ANTIPHO: Oh if only he will!

GETA: He will, trust me. Now here's your father coming out – run along and tell Phaedria the money's there.

[ANTIPHO *hurries off right as* CHREMES *and* DEMIPHO *come out of* CHREMES' *house with the promised money.*]

DEMIPHO: Don't worry, I tell you. I'll see he doesn't cheat us. I'll take care not to hand over the cash except in the presence of a witness, and when I do so I shall state exactly what it's for.

GETA [*aside*]: Cautious, isn't he, now there's no need.

CHREMES: That's the way to do it, but do hurry up before his mood changes. If the other girl puts pressure on him he may turn us down.

GETA [*aside*]: How right you are!

DEMIPHO: Geta! Take me to him.

GETA: I'm ready, sir.

CHREMES: When you've finished, come over to my wife and ask her to see the girl before she leaves you and tell her we're arranging a marriage with Phormio and she's not to be annoyed. He's more her sort and a better match for her, and we've done our duty by her – he's having all the dowry he asked for.

DEMIPHO [*exasperated*]: What the hell does this matter to you?

CHREMES: It matters a lot, Demipho. Doing your duty isn't enough unless people know and approve. I want Phanium's consent to this so that she won't go around saying she was turned out of your house.

DEMIPHO: I can do it just as well myself.

CHREMES: Women are better at handling women.

DEMIPHO: All right, I'll ask her.

[*He goes off right with* GETA.]

CHREMES: And now I'm wondering where I can find the other two.

[*The old nurse,* SOPHRONA, *comes out of* DEMIPHO'S *house to give voice to her troubles.*]

SOPHRONA: What shall I do? Oh dear, dear, where can I find a friend? Where can I tell my tale and seek help? I'm so afraid my mistress will be terribly wronged – and all through taking my advice. It seems the young man's father is furious at what we've done.

CHREMES: Who on earth is this old woman bursting out of my brother's house in such a state?

SOPHRONA: It was our poverty which drove me to it. I knew this marriage wasn't secure but I had to provide for her somehow while we waited –

CHREMES: Unless my eyes deceive me and my mind is giving
way I do believe I see my daughter's nurse!

SOPHRONA: And now there's no trace –

CHREMES: What shall I do –

SOPHRONA: – of her father.

CHREMES: – go up to her or wait until she says something
which makes more sense?

SOPHRONA: If only I could find him I'd have nothing to fear.

CHREMES: It *is* the nurse. I'll speak to her.

SOPHRONA [*aware at last that she is not alone*]: Who's that?

CHREMES: Sophrona!

SOPHRONA: And he knows my name!

CHREMES: Turn round.

SOPHRONA: Heavens above, it's Stilpo!

CHREMES: No, no.

SOPHRONA: Did you say No?

CHREMES [*nervously*]: Come over here, please Sophrona, a
little further from the door. . . . Don't ever call me by that
name again.

SOPHRONA: Why? Aren't you the man you always said you
were?

CHREMES: Sh . . .

SOPHRONA: Why are you afraid of this door?

CHREMES: I've a wife behind it – a dangerous one. And that
was a false name I gave you before, in case any of you were
careless enough to let out the real one and my wife found
out.

SOPHRONA: So that's why we poor women could never find
you here!

CHREMES [*anxious to change the subject*]: Now please tell me
why you came out of that door. Do you know the family?
And where are – the others?

SOPHRONA [*tearfully*]: Oh dear . . .

CHREMES: What's the matter? Are they alive?

SOPHRONA: The daughter is. The mother, poor soul, died of the distress you caused her.

CHREMES: That's bad. . . .

SOPHRONA: And I was left here, a penniless old woman without a friend, but I did what I could. I married the girl to the young gentleman who is master of this house.

CHREMES: To Antipho?

SOPHRONA: Yes, to him.

CHREMES [*obtusely*]: What! Has he *two* wives?

SOPHRONA: Good heavens no, sir, he only has this one.

CHREMES: What about the other one who's called his relative?

SOPHRONA: That's her.

CHREMES: *What* do you say?

SOPHRONA: It was all a put-up job, sir, so that her lover could marry her without a dowry.

CHREMES: Ye gods, how often chance brings about more than we dare to hope! I've come back to find my daughter happily married to the man I wanted and the very way I wanted! He has achieved by his own unaided efforts – with no help from us – the very thing my brother and I were trying so hard to bring about.

SOPHRONA: Now think what we must do, sir; the young man's father is here and they say he's very much put out.

CHREMES: Oh, there's no danger there, but I'd move heaven and earth to stop anyone knowing she's my daughter.

SOPHRONA: No one shall learn it from *me*.

CHREMES: Come with me: I'll tell you the rest of the story indoors.

[*They go into* DEMIPHO's *house; soon after* DEMIPHO *and* GETA *return, right.*]

DEMIPHO: Well, we've only ourselves to blame if we allow dishonesty to pay just by being too careful to preserve our own reputation for generosity and fair dealing. We shouldn't overshoot the mark, as the saying goes. It was bad enough to have to swallow the man's insults without paying him cash into the bargain. Now he's got something to live on while he's plotting fresh wickedness.

GETA: Quite so, sir.

DEMIPHO: Nowadays the rewards go for putting the straight crooked –

GETA: Too true.

DEMIPHO: – and we've been a pair of fools.

GETA: Let's hope the plan comes off and he really does marry her.

DEMIPHO: Why, is there any doubt about it?

GETA: Well, being human, he might change his mind. . . .

DEMIPHO: But surely he won't?

GETA: I don't know, sir, I only said he might.

DEMIPHO: I'll do as my brother advised and ask his wife to talk to the girl. Go on ahead, Geta, and tell her that Nausistrata is coming.

[*He goes into* CHREMES' *house to fetch her.*]

GETA: We've got the cash for Phaedria, and his quarrel's settled. For the moment Phanium won't leave us, but what about the future? What'll happen? You're stuck in the same mud, Geta; you'll have to repay a new loan. You can put off the evil day for a while, but look out – the blows are mounting up. Well, I'm off home to tell Phanium she needn't fear Phormio or anything he says.

[*He goes into* DEMIPHO's *house as* DEMIPHO *comes out of* CHREMES' *house with* NAUSISTRATA.]

DEMIPHO: Now, Nausistrata, use your powers of persuasion

to make her agree to what we want, and accept of her own
accord what has to be.

NAUSISTRATA: I will.

DEMIPHO: Your support can help me as much now as your
money did before.

NAUSISTRATA: I'm glad, and if I can't do as much as I should
it's my husband's fault.

DEMIPHO: What do you mean?

NAUSISTRATA: Chremes is so careless in the way he handles
my father's properties. *He* used to make twelve thousand
drachmas regularly out of those farms. What a difference
there is between one man and another!

DEMIPHO: Did you say twelve thousand?

NAUSISTRATA: Yes, twelve thousand, and prices were much
lower then.

DEMIPHO [*indicates astonishment*]

NAUSISTRATA: What do you think of that?

DEMIPHO [*not listening*]: Yes, yes, of course.

NAUSISTRATA: I wish I'd been born a man: I'd have shown
him –

DEMIPHO: I'm sure you would.

NAUSISTRATA: – just how –

DEMIPHO: Not now, please, save your strength for the girl,
she's young and may tire you.

NAUSISTRATA: I'll do what you want. [*She turns to go as*
CHREMES *comes out in a state of great excitement.*] Why,
there's my husband coming out of your house.

CHREMES [*not seeing* NAUSISTRATA]: I say, Demipho, have
you paid him the money yet?

DEMIPHO: Yes, I did it at once.

CHREMES: I wish you hadn't. [*Aside*] Dear me, there's my
wife. I nearly said too much.

DEMIPHO: Why do you wish I hadn't?

CHREMES: It's all right now.

DEMIPHO: What about you? Have you said anything to the girl about your wife's coming to see her?

CHREMES: It's all settled.

DEMIPHO: What does she say then?

CHREMES: The move's off.

DEMIPHO: Why on earth?

CHREMES [*searching for a reason*]: Because ... they're in love.

DEMIPHO: What's that got to do with it?

CHREMES: A lot. [*Trying not to let* NAUSISTRATA *hear*] Besides, I've discovered she *is* related to me.

DEMIPHO: What? You're crazy.

CHREMES: You'll see. I'm not just talking. I've remembered something.

DEMIPHO [*mystified*]: Are you out of your mind?

NAUSISTRATA [*equally at sea*]: Now don't you be wronging a relative!

DEMIPHO: She isn't one.

CHREMES: Don't be so sure. Her father's name was wrongly given and that misled you.

DEMIPHO: Doesn't she know her own father?

CHREMES: Of course she does.

DEMIPHO: Then why get his name wrong?

CHREMES [*in a frantic whisper*]: Will you please drop this at once and try to understand what I'm saying?

DEMIPHO: But you don't talk sense.

CHREMES: Oh, you'll be the death of me.

NAUSISTRATA: I wonder what this is all about!

DEMIPHO: Don't ask me.

CHREMES [*still trying to take him aside*]: If you really want to know – God help me, there's no one so nearly related to her as we two are.

DEMIPHO: Then for Heaven's sake let's go and find her and all be present to see if you're right about this – or not.

CHREMES: Sh . . .

DEMIPHO: What?

CHREMES: Can't you trust me a little more?

DEMIPHO: You want me to take your word for it? And stop asking questions? Oh, all right. But what about the daughter of that friend of ours? What's to become of her?

CHREMES: That's all right.

DEMIPHO: Are we giving up that plan?

CHREMES: Yes, yes.

DEMIPHO: And the other one's to stay?

CHREMES: Yes.

DEMIPHO: Then we needn't keep you, Nausistrata.

NAUSISTRATA [*trying to conceal her incomprehension*]: I'm sure it's best for everyone that she should stay, after all. She seemed a very lady-like girl when I saw her.

[*She goes back into* CHREMES' *house.*]

DEMIPHO: *Now*, Chremes; what's all this about?

CHREMES: Has she shut the door?

DEMIPHO: Yes.

CHREMES [*relaxing*]: Praise Heaven, the gods are on our side! The girl your son married – I find she's my own daughter!

DEMIPHO: How can she be?

CHREMES: It isn't safe to tell you out here.

DEMIPHO: Well then, come indoors.

CHREMES: Listen, I don't want even our sons to know this. . . .

[*They go into* DEMIPHO'S *house; soon after,* ANTIPHO *returns, right, from his meeting with* PHAEDRIA.]

ANTIPHO: Whatever happens to me, I'm glad my cousin has

got what he wants. How sensible people are who set their
hearts on things which can easily be put right if they go
wrong! Phaedria had only to find the cash to be rid of his
worries, but look at me – I can't see any way of extricating
myself from my troubles. If the secret's kept I live in appre-
hension, and if it comes out I'm disgraced. I shouldn't be
going home now if there weren't some hope I can keep my
wife. . . . I wish I could find Geta, to ask what he thinks is
the best moment to approach my father.

[PHORMIO *comes on right, voicing his satisfaction without
seeing* ANTIPHO.]

PHORMIO: I got the money, paid it to the pimp, removed the
girl, and saw that Phaedria took her for his own now she's
been freed. Now I've only one more thing to do to be rid
of the old men and have some peace for a drink – I'm
thinking of taking a few days off.

ANTIPHO [*coming to meet him*]: Why, it's Phormio. Tell me –

PHORMIO: Yes?

ANTIPHO: What's Phaedria going to do now? How does he
propose to take his fill of his love?

PHORMIO: He's going to take a turn at your part –

ANTIPHO: Which one?

PHORMIO: – and hide from his father. He asks you to take
over his, and plead his case, while he comes over to my
house for a drink. I shall tell the old men I'm off to the fair
at Sunium to buy the maid Geta spoke of just now, for if
they don't see me around they'll imagine I'm running
through their money. That sounded like your door.

ANTIPHO: See who it is.

PHORMIO: It's Geta.

[GETA *bursts out in a state of incoherent excitement.*]

GETA: O Fortune, divine Fortune, what blessings you have

heaped on my master Antipho, now, this very day, with your divine aid –

ANTIPHO: What on earth does he mean?

GETA: And rid us, his friends, of all our fears! Quick, make ready, be off to find him, tell him his good luck!

ANTIPHO: Do you understand what he's saying?

PHORMIO: Do you?

ANTIPHO: Not a word.

PHORMIO: No more do I.

GETA: I'll try Dorio's; they must be there [*setting off towards* DORIO's *house.*]

ANTIPHO: Hi, Geta!

GETA [*not looking back*]: There you are; the usual thing, called back as soon as you've set off.

ANTIPHO: Geta!

GETA: How that fellow carries on. A proper nuisance, but he won't stop *me*.

ANTIPHO: Please wait.

GETA: Go hang yourself!

ANTIPHO: Exactly what'll happen to you if you don't stop, you rascal.

GETA: He must be one of the family, threatening me like this. Can it be the man I'm looking for? I do believe it is. Quick, come here, sir.

ANTIPHO: What is it?

GETA [*ecstatically*]: O man most fortunate of all men alive! Beyond dispute, sir, you're the true beloved of the gods!

ANTIPHO: I wish I were. And I wish someone would tell me why I'm to believe you.

GETA: Suppose I drown you deep in delight? Would that satisfy you?

ANTIPHO: Oh, you make me tired!

PHORMIO: Stop holding forth and give us the news.

GETA [*affecting surprise*]: You here too, Phormio?

PHORMIO: Yes. Hurry up.

GETA: All right, listen. When we'd met you in town and handed over the money we came straight back home. Presently my master sent me across to your wife.

ANTIPHO: What for?

GETA: I'm not going into that, sir, it's beside the point. I was just going into the women's quarters when the boy Mida ran up, caught hold of me and pulled me back. I looked round and asked why he was stopping me. He said his orders were no admission to his mistress. Sophrona had just taken in the master's brother, Chremes, and he was still in there with them. When I heard this, I tiptoed softly to the door, reached it, stood close with my ear to the crack, holding my breath, and listened hard – like this – to catch what was said.

PHORMIO: Bravo, Geta!

GETA: This way I heard something simply wonderful, and very nearly cried out for joy.

ANTIPHO: What was it?

GETA: Can you guess?

ANTIPHO: I've no idea.

GETA: It's really marvellous. It's now known that your uncle is the father of your wife Phanium.

ANTIPHO: I don't believe you.

GETA: He had a secret affair with her mother years ago in Lemnos.

PHORMIO: Nonsense! How was it she didn't know her own father?

GETA: There's a reason for that, Phormio, believe me. Anyway, I was outside the door. Do you suppose I could follow every word they were saying?

ANTIPHO: Besides, I remember now hearing a rumour about it.

GETA: What's more, here's something to convince you. Presently your uncle came out here, and soon afterwards went in again with your father. Both of them said you could have her for your wife. And finally, I've been sent to find you and take you in.

ANTIPHO: Then hurry, can't you. What are you waiting for?

GETA [*as he hustles him into* DEMIPHO'S *house*]: There you are!

ANTIPHO: Good-bye, Phormio!

PHORMIO: Good-bye, Antipho. This is lovely; I'm delighted. [ANTIPHO *and* GETA *go in.*] What an unexpected stroke of good luck for those two! And a splendid opportunity for me to diddle the old men and rid Phaedria of his money worries before he has to go begging to his friends. The money's been paid over and it's not being handed back, whether the old men like it or not; in fact I know how I can put pressure on them. Now I'll play a new part: I'll just slip down the nearest side-street and appear when they come out. I can give up the idea of pretending to go to Sunium. [*He hurries off, right, as* CHREMES *and* DEMIPHO *come out of the house.*]

DEMIPHO: Well, brother, things have turned out well for us, thank God; I'm truly and properly grateful. Now we must be quick and find Phormio, and recover our three thousand before he squanders the lot.

PHORMIO [*reappearing*]: I'll just see if Demipho's at home, so that –

DEMIPHO: Why, we were coming to see you, Phormio.

PHORMIO: On the same old errand, I suppose?

DEMIPHO: That's right.

PHORMIO: I thought as much. Now I wonder *why* you wanted me?

DEMIPHO: Don't be silly.

PHORMIO: Were you afraid that I shouldn't carry out my promise? Kindly note that though my means may be of the smallest, I have always endeavoured to be a man of my word.

CHREMES [*sarcastically*]: Didn't I tell you he was the perfect gentleman?

DEMIPHO: Quite so.

PHORMIO: I am on my way now, Demipho, to tell you I am ready; you can hand my bride over any time you like. I postponed all my personal affairs, as was only proper, when I saw you were both so anxious for this marriage.

DEMIPHO: But my brother here has persuaded me not to give her to you; he reminds me what people will say if I do. I didn't do so at the time when I could have done without loss of reputation, and to turn her out of the house now would create a scandal. In fact, his arguments are much the same as the ones you used against me yourself earlier on.

PHORMIO: You can't make a fool of me in this high-handed way!

DEMIPHO: What do you mean?

PHORMIO: You know very well I shan't be able to marry the other girl either. I should never have the face to go back after I treated her so badly.

CHREMES [*prompting* DEMIPHO]: And now you find that Antipho is unwilling to part with her.

DEMIPHO: And now I find my son is most unwilling to part with his wife. Please come across to the bank and have the money transferred back into my account.

PHORMIO: But I've already drawn it to pay my debts.

DEMIPHO [*at a loss*]: What are we to do then?

HORMIO [*with injured dignity*]: If you intend to give me the
bride you promised, Demipho, I will marry her; but if you
really wish her to stay with you, I shall keep the dowry. It
is not right that I should be cheated on your account,
gentlemen, especially as it was to safeguard your position
that I broke with a girl who was going to bring me the same
sum.

DEMIPHO: Go to hell with your high and mighty airs, you
miserable creature! Do you imagine we don't know you
and your doings?

HORMIO: Don't provoke me.

DEMIPHO: Would you marry her if she were offered you?

HORMIO: Try me!

DEMIPHO: This is all a plot between you and Antipho; he's
going to live with her in your house!

HORMIO: What *are* you talking about?

DEMIPHO: Hand over my money!

HORMIO: Hand over my wife!

DEMIPHO [*seizing him*]: Then come to court –

HORMIO [*disengaging himself*]: If you people continue to be so
offensive –

DEMIPHO: What will you do?

HORMIO [*meaningly*]: Aha! Maybe you think it's only penniless girls whose cause I champion. . . . Well, I'm interested
in women of property too.

CHREMES: That's no concern of ours.

HORMIO: No, no concern at all. [*Slowly*] I knew a lady here
whose husband had –

CHREMES: What?

HORMIO: – another wife in Lemnos –

CHREMES [*aside*]: I'm done for.

PHORMIO: – by whom he had a daughter. He brought the
girl up secretly. . . .

CHREMES [*aside*]: It's the end of me.

PHORMIO [*with relish*]: And that's the story I intend to tell to
her [*indicating* CHREMES' *house*] in – all – its – details.

CHREMES: No, no, please don't.

PHORMIO: Well, well. Could you be that man?

DEMIPHO: He's only fooling.

CHREMES: We'll let you off.

PHORMIO: Rubbish!

CHREMES: What do you want for yourself? We'll make you
a present of the money in your possession.

PHORMIO: And I'll accept your offer. What the devil do you
mean, putting me off with all this shilly-shallying like a pair
of stupid children? 'I won't, I will: then, I will, I won't;
take it, give it back; take what's said as unsaid, cancel what
was just agreed.'

　　[*He turns to go.*]

CHREMES [*to* DEMIPHO]: How did he find out? Who told
him?

DEMIPHO: I've no idea. I only know I told no one.

CHREMES: Damn it all, it's uncanny.

PHORMIO [*aside*]: That's stung them.

DEMIPHO: But is this man to have the laugh on us quite
openly and make off with all that cash? I'd rather die. Just
you be a man and show some presence of mind. You can
see your misdeeds are out and can't be kept from your wife:
she's bound to hear the news from someone, and it would
be easier to placate her if we told her ourselves. Then we
can deal with this filthy brute in our own way.

PHORMIO [*aside*]: I'm caught if I don't look out. Once their
blood's up they'll round on me in desperation.

CHREMES: But I very much doubt if she *can* be placated.

DEMIPHO: Courage, Chremes. I'll see you're reconciled. After all, the girl's mother is out of the way.

PHORMIO [*coming back*]: Is this how you treat me? Artful pair, aren't you. My God, Demipho, you don't do your brother much good, trying my patience like this. Well, Chremes: you took your pleasure abroad, without scruple or thought for your excellent wife to restrain you from insulting her in this outrageous fashion. Are you coming now with prayers on your lips to expiate your sins? I've something to tell her which will spark off such a blaze of fury that you'll never put it out, not even if you dissolve into tears.

DEMIPHO: May all the powers of heaven see him damned! I never heard of such colossal cheek. The state should have him deported – a desert island's the place for criminals like him.

CHREMES [*hopelessly*]: I'm reduced to such a state I can't think *what* to do with him.

DEMIPHO: I know; let's take him to court.

PHORMIO [*insolently*]: Certainly; set up court in there [*moving to* CHREMES' *house*].

CHREMES: After him, hold him, while I call out the servants!

DEMIPHO [*seizing* PHORMIO]: I can't by myself – quick, come and help me!

PHORMIO [*struggling*]: I'll have the law on you for assault!

DEMIPHO: All right, you can.

PHORMIO [*as* CHREMES *catches hold of him*]: And on you, Chremes.

CHREMES: Take him off –

PHORMIO: Oh, would you. Very well, I'll try shouting. Nausistrata! Come out!

CHREMES [*frantically*]: Shut your dirty mouth! Oh, how strong he is.

PHORMIO: Nausistrata!

DEMIPHO: Be quiet.

PHORMIO: Why should I?

DEMIPHO: If he won't come, punch him in the belly.

PHORMIO: Knock an eye out if you like. There's a proper punishment coming to you – both of you.

[*He struggles free as* NAUSISTRATA *comes out of* CHREMES' *house.*]

NAUSISTRATA: Who's calling me? Goodness me, Chremes, what's all this about?

PHORMIO [*triumphantly*]: Aha! Struck dumb now, are you?

NAUSISTRATA: Who's that man? Why don't you answer me?

PHORMIO: How can he answer you? He doesn't know where he is.

CHREMES [*his teeth chattering with fright*]: D-don't you b-believe a word he says.

PHORMIO: Go on, touch him. Strike me dead if you don't find him frozen stiff.

CHREMES [*trying to control himself*]: It's n-nothing.

NAUSISTRATA: Then what is it? What's he talking about?

PHORMIO: You'll soon know; just listen.

CHREMES: Must you believe him?

NAUSISTRATA: How can I believe him when he hasn't spoken yet?

PHORMIO: Poor creature, he's crazed with fear.

NAUSISTRATA: There must be something wrong, to frighten you like this.

CHREMES: Who says I'm frightened?

PHORMIO: That's a good one! No, you're not frightened, and there's nothing in what I say – so *you* tell her.

DEMIPHO: Not at your bidding, you scoundrel!

PHORMIO: Now, now, Demipho, you've done a good job for your brother.

NAUSISTRATA: Chremes, please won't you tell me?

CHREMES: But –

NAUSISTRATA: But what?

CHREMES: There's nothing to tell.

PHORMIO: Nothing to tell *you*, maybe; but *she* should know. In Lemnos –

DEMIPHO: Look here –

CHREMES: Will you be quiet?

PHORMIO: – unknown to you –

CHREMES [*aside*]: O woe!

PHORMIO: – he married a wife.

NAUSISTRATA: My good man, you must be crazy.

PHORMIO: It's the truth.

NAUSISTRATA: No, no, I can't bear it.

PHORMIO: Then he had a daughter by her. Still you knew nothing.

CHREMES: What are we to do?

NAUSISTRATA: Gracious heavens, what a monstrous, wicked thing!

PHORMIO [*to* CHREMES]: Do? Nothing. It's too late.

NAUSISTRATA: It's cruelly unfair! It's only when they're with their *wives* that men can remember their age. Demipho, I appeal to you; I'm too disgusted to speak to him. Is this the explanation of all those journeys and long visits to Lemnos? Are these the low prices which reduced my profits?

DEMIPHO [*uncomfortably*]: I'm not denying he's to blame in this, Nausistrata, but perhaps you should forgive him –

PHORMIO: Famous last words!

DEMIPHO: He didn't do anything out of disregard or dislike of you. It all happened about fifteen years ago, when he was drunk. ... He met this woman, and then the girl was born ... but he never touched her after that. Now she's dead, which takes away a lot of the difficulty, so I do beg you to show your usual good sense and take this calmly.

NAUSISTRATA: How can I take it calmly? I should like to see the end of my troubles in this sorry matter, but what hope have I of doing so? Are advancing years likely to improve his future behaviour? If old age makes men respectable – well, he wasn't young *then*. Am I younger now and more attractive than I was at that time? What reason can you give, Demipho, for me to have better hopes and expectations for the future?

PHORMIO [*to the audience*]: All who should attend Chremes' funeral kindly note the time has come! Now then: anyone want to challenge Phormio? All right, let him come. I'll see he suffers the same punishment as Chremes. Very well, restore him to favour; my vengeance is satisfied. His wife'll have something to whine about in his ear for the rest of his life.

NAUSISTRATA: I suppose he'll say I deserve this? Have I to start now and tell you in detail all I've been to him?

DEMIPHO: No, no, I know it all as well as you do.

NAUSISTRATA: And do you think I deserve this?

DEMIPHO: Certainly not. But you can't mend matters by this sort of accusation, so you'd best forgive him. He confesses, apologizes and begs for mercy. What more do you want?

PHORMIO [*aside*]: Quick, she's going to forgive him – I must look out for myself and Phaedria. [*Aloud*] Madam, before you give a hasty answer, please listen to me.

NAUSISTRATA: What is it?

PHORMIO [*with emphasis*]: I tricked your husband out of three thousand drachmas and gave them to Phaedria. He's already paid them over to the pimp to buy the girl who's his mistress.

CHREMES: What's that you're saying?

NAUSISTRATA [*icily*]: Surely you can't blame your son for keeping a single mistress when you have two wives? Oh, you're shameless! Have you really the face to rebuke him? Answer me.

DEMIPHO [*hastily*]: Chremes will do anything you like.

NAUSISTRATA: No; first you can hear what *I* have to say. I don't forgive you, Chremes, and I'm making no promises and giving no answers until I've seen Phaedria. Everything rests on his decision; I shall do what he advises.

PHORMIO: You're a wise woman, Madam.

NAUSISTRATA: Does that satisfy you?

PHORMIO: Yes indeed. I'm getting off lightly, much better than I expected.

NAUSISTRATA: Please tell me your name.

PHORMIO: My name's Phormio: a good friend of the family, and a very good one to your son Phaedria.

NAUSISTRATA: Phormio, from now on I will say and do anything I can to further your wishes.

PHORMIO: You're very kind.

NAUSISTRATA: No more than you deserve.

PHORMIO: Would you like to begin today, Madam, and do something which will be a pleasure to me – *and* a slap in the eye for your husband?

NAUSISTRATA: I certainly would.

PHORMIO: Then invite me to dinner.

NAUSISTRATA: Of course; I invite you now.

DEMIPHO: Let us go in then.

NAUSISTRATA: We're coming. But where's Phaedria? I'm
   waiting for his opinion.
PHORMIO: I'll fetch him at once.
   [PHORMIO *goes off right, to his house, where* PHAEDRIA *is
   hiding;* DEMIPHO *escorts* NAUSISTRATA *into her house;*
   CHREMES, *quite ignored, slowly follows them.*]

BIBLIOGRAPHY

Alkins, J. W. H., *Literary Criticism in Antiquity* (1934).

Beare, W., *The Roman Stage* (third edition, revised, 1964).

Bieber, M., *The History of the Greek and Roman Theater* (second edition, 1961).

Bolgar, R. R., *The Classical Heritage* (1954).

Chassang, A., *Des Essais dramatiques imités de l'Antiquité* (1852).

Diderot, D., *Réflexions sur Térence* (1762).

Duckworth, G. E., *The Nature of Roman Comedy* (1951).

Frank, Tenney, *Life and Literature in the Roman Republic* (1930).

Graves, R., ed., Echard's translation (1689) of *The Comedies of Terence* (1963).

Highet, G., *The Classical Tradition* (1949).

Lawton, H. W., *Térence en France au XVIe siècle* (1926).

Marouzeau, J., *Térence, texte établi et traduit* (Budé edition, 1947).

Martin, R. H., ed., *Phormio* (1959).

Meredith, G., *An Essay on Comedy* (1877).

Molière, *Les Fourberies de Scapin*, tr. John Wood in *The Miser and Other Plays* (Penguin Classics, 1953).

Norwood, G., *The Art of Terence* (1923).

Radice, B., tr., Terence, *The Brothers and Other Plays* (Penguin Classics, 1965).

Sainte-Beuve, *Nouveaux Lundis* (3 and 10 August 1863).

Sandys, J. E., *A History of Classical Scholarship* (1903).

Sargeaunt, J., *Annals of Westminster School* (1898).

Sargeaunt, J., ed., *The Plays of Terence* (Loeb edition, 1912).

Sellar, W. Y., *Roman Poets of the Republic* (1889).

Shipp, G. P., ed., *Andria* (1960).

Vellacott, P., tr., *Menander and Theophrastus* (Penguin Classics, 1967).

Watling, E. F., tr., Plautus, *The Rope and Other Plays* (Penguin Classics, 1964).

Watling, E. F., tr., Plautus, *The Pot of Gold and Other Plays* (Penguin Classics, 1965).

Webster, T. B. L., *Studies in Menander* (1949).

KING ALFRED'S COLLEGE

LIBRARY

MORE ABOUT PENGUINS

If you have enjoyed reading this book you may wish to know that *Penguin Book News* appears every month. It is an attractively illustrated magazine containing a complete list of books published by Penguins and still in print, together with details of the month's new books. A specimen copy will be sent free on request.

Penguin Book News is obtainable from most bookshops; but you may prefer to become a regular subscriber at 3s. for twelve issues. Just write to Dept EP, Penguin Books Ltd, Harmondsworth, Middlesex, enclosing a cheque or postal order, and you will be put on the mailing list.

Some other Penguin Classics are described on the following pages.

Note: *Penguin Book News* is not
available in the U.S.A., Canada or Australia

PENGUIN CLASSICS

JUVENAL
THE SIXTEEN SATIRES
Translated by Peter Green

The splendour, squalor, and complexity of the Roman scene were never more vividly presented than by the satirist Juvenal (c. A.D. 55–130). His bitter and forcible verses were written during the reigns of Trajan and Hadrian, which Gibbon (from a safe distance) called 'the period in the history of the world during which the condition of the human race was most happy and prosperous'. To quote Peter Green's introduction, 'Juvenal does not work out a coherent ethical critique of institutions or individuals: he simply hangs a series of moral portraits on the wall and forces us to look at them'.

THE PENGUIN CLASSICS

THE MOST RECENT VOLUMES

KING HARALD'S SAGA
Magnus Magnusson and Hermann Pálsson

BASHŌ
The Narrow Road to the Deep North and Other Travel
Sketches
Nobuyuki Yuasa

TOLSTOY
Resurrection · *Rosemary Edmonds*

TURGENEV
Sketches From a Hunter's Album · *Richard Freeborn*

★ODES OF HORACE · *James Michie*

FONTANE
Effi Briest · *Douglas Parmée*

CAESAR
The Civil War · *Jane F. Mitchell*

MENANDER
Plays and Fragments · *Philip Vellacott*

THEOPHRASTUS
The Characters

JUVENAL
The Sixteen Satires · *Peter Green*

★ *Not for sale in the U.S.A. or Canada*